DEVOTIONAL TALKS ON EVERYDAY OBJECTS

Devotional Talks
on Everyday Objects

Robert J. Hastings

BROADMAN PRESS
Nashville, Tennessee

Dewey Decimal Classification Number: 268.7
Library of Congress Catalog Card Number: 68–26919
Printed in the United States of America
7.5F6814

PREFACE

Here are twenty-seven "attention-getters" for persons
called on to give devotionals or lead worship programs for
any age group. These are more than the usual object lessons
—they are devices to capture the attention of your group as
you relate a simple, everyday article to a basic spiritual
truth.

Follow these helpful suggestions:

1. You may use these in a series, or select one or two for
occasional use.

2. They are helpful for any age group. With younger ages,
you can simplify the application. With older groups, you can
enlarge on the author's suggestions.

3. The suggested articles or objects are easy for you to
find in your own home. In very few instances will you need
to buy anything.

4. Use your own creativity and imagination to enlarge on
the author's ideas. Take the first program on medicine bottles, for example. You might think of labels other than those
mentioned and come up with something even more appeal-
ing.

5. These ideas can be used in assembly programs, mid-
week services, class meetings, men's meetings, with children's

groups, or on any occasion when you want something a little different to capture attention.

6. If you involve your listeners, they will show even more interest. You may use them to collect the objects, arrange them before the service, assist you in the presentation, or in other ways.

CONTENTS

1 Follow Directions!

Preparation: Get five medicine bottles of various sizes and shapes. These could be old bottles from your medicine cabinet, or borrowed from a neighbor. Be sure to empty the contents. Ask your druggist for five blank labels (he will probably give them to you). On each label type or letter by hand one of the "prescriptions" listed below. You may stick the labels to the bottles in advance and have them on display for the worship service, or you may distribute the labels to five persons who will come forward at the appropriate time and stick them to the bottles. The larger the group, the larger the bottles should be. A tiny bottle could hardly be seen in a large group.

"Take Only As Directed"

Who would be so foolish as to take medicine from a bottle without first reading the directions? Yet all of us have seen persons who are so anxious to "get on with the living" that they never wait to ask the advice of others who have more experience. If it could be harmful to take even one tablet

1

without first reading the directions, how much more harmful might it be to make decisions about our friends, church, habits, future, life work, or marriage without some kind of directions? For such "directions," we can turn to parents, an older friend, a trusted pastor, a favorite teacher, a guidance counselor, a physician, or a psychiatrist.

For the Christian there is another source of direction. Proverbs 3:6 says, "In all thy ways acknowledge him, and he shall direct thy paths." We should never hesitate to ask God for direction, for wisdom, for help.

"One Tablet Before Each Meal"

Psalm 55:17 says, "Evening, and morning, and at noon, will I pray, and cry aloud: and he shall hear my voice." Many families pause for prayer at mealtime. Whether we are in a crowded restaurant, a drive-in, or the family kitchen, mealtime can be a reminder to us to turn our thoughts toward God. Although prayer should never become a routine, to form the habit of at least three "doses" a day is helpful. As we approach each meal, let us at least breathe a prayer of thanks, of praise, of repentance, as we pray for guidance through the remainder of the day.

"A Tablespoon at Bedtime"

One of the best preparations for bedtime is to free our minds of all bad thoughts and worries. Ephesians 4:26 prescribes, "Let not the sun go down upon your wrath." Some people can't sleep at night because they are angry, jealous, or afraid. Just as it is a good idea to brush one's teeth and wash one's face before going to bed, so it is good to wash our minds of the ill feelings we might have toward someone. We will sleep better, and be rested for the new day.

"Poison—Do Not Take Internally"

Some medicines, such as alcohol or liniment, are for external use only. If we drink them, death or serious illness may result. When we see "Poison" on a bottle, we should keep it (like all medicines) out of reach of small children, and in a safe place so that we will not accidentally take it during the night.

The Bible has a warning about poison in 1 Thessalonians 5:22: "Abstain from all appearance of evil." The Christian is to avoid whatever appears to be wrong, even on the outside. His attitude is not, "How much evil can I do and still get by?" Rather, it is, "What is the least possible wrong that I can do and still be human?"

"Caution—May Be Habit-forming"

There are some drugs which do not kill or make us seriously ill but which, over a period of time, will damage our physical and emotional health. There are times when, on the doctor's prescription, we can benefit from these. But if we continue to depend on these for a crutch after the immediate need is past, they may become habit-forming and damaging. A simple example is talking about other people. If we refused to say *anything* about other people, there would be little to talk about. But we can go too far. We can pry for faults in others, and then scatter and enlarge those faults. Before long, we may fall into destructive gossip, an almost unbreakable habit once it gets a foothold.

Hymns: "More Like the Master"
           "Jesus, the Very Thought of Thee"
           "I Would Be True"

Prayer: Father God, give us the desire to seek thy help, the
           wisdom to understand it, the patience to use it, and
           the courage to follow it. In the name of Christ.
           Amen.

2 Let's Go for a Drive

Preparation: You will need five highway signs, or replicas. A friend in the state highway department may loan them, or someone in your city street department. Real signs will attract more attention. But if this is impossible, make your own signs on poster board. Fasten them to stands or posts, and have them on display as your group assembles. Or you might line them up near the door to catch attention, and later move them to the front of the room or department. Someone in your class or department might help you make the signs. Make them as authentic-looking as possible, using the standard highway colors of your state.

Stop

The most familiar of all signs is that which reads "Stop." Millions and millions of these familiar signs dot the streets and highways of our nation. If any one sign should be obeyed, this is it! It is just as important to know how to stop a car as it is to start one. A person may know how to use the accelerator, but unless he also knows how to use the brake, he should never start a car.

The function of a stop sign is to give us time to see if the way is clear. A stop sign does not mean the end of a trip or a drive. It simply means that we are to make sure the way is clear before proceeding. In your personal life, do you ever take time to stop and think about the direction you are headed? Do you pause long enough to see if the course you are following is a wise one, to see if there are any obstacles in the way?

One purpose of prayer is to ask, "Lord, am I headed right?" Often we stop long enough to ask a friend, "What is your opinion about what I am trying to do?" Quiet meditation, when we are alone with our thoughts, is another good "stop sign" that helps us think through our problems rather than go blindly onward.

Dangerous Intersection

A danger sign is used to warn of sharp curves, steep hills, railroad crossings, and dangerous intersections. This sign alerts us to watch for the unexpected. It says that a normal driving pattern will not do for the emergency that might arise. Extra caution is called for.

In our personal lives, we do not always know when these unexpected crises may come. Often there is no warning sign. What are some of these out-of-the routine events? Sudden illness. Death of a loved one. A move to a new community. A new baby. A new boyfriend. A wedding. A divorce. War. Loss of job. All of these are crises because they mark a change in the regular routine of our lives. They demand more from us. They can work for the good or the bad, depending to some degree on our attitude.

Two-Way Traffic

All of us have had the experience of driving on an interstate highway, where we meet no oncoming traffic, and then seeing the sign "Two-Way Traffic Ahead." This tells us that we are shifting from the higher-speed, one-way traffic pattern to a narrower highway where we may encounter oncoming cars. Two-way traffic requires more alertness and is usually more frustrating and dangerous.

Translated into everyday life, this sign means, "You can't have the whole road to yourself." We know what a road hog is. We don't like them. But not all road hogs are found on highways. They may be found wherever there are people living and working together—in homes, churches, schools, playgrounds, offices, mines, and plants. A road hog is one who thinks of no one but himself. First Corinthians 8:13 is a good verse for anyone with road-hog tendencies: "Wherefore, if meat make my brother to offend, I will eat no flesh while the world standeth, lest I make my brother to offend." The meaning is simple. One never makes a decision without its affecting someone else. We ought to consider the feelings and ideas and tastes and preferences of others.

One-Way Street

This is the exact opposite of the "Two-Way Traffic" sign. It tells us that all traffic is moving in the same direction. We must keep going in the direction we are headed. We cannot stop and turn around. We may not like the way we are headed, but we must stay in that traffic pattern, at least temporarily.

There are times in life when we get tired, or dissatisfied, or restless. This may occur in our Christian life, as we serve in our church. If so, it is time to obey Luke 9:62: "No man, having put his hand to the plough, and looking back, is fit for the kingdom of God." This does not mean we should never consider another direction in life. It does mean, however, that the fellow who is constantly changing his mind, who finds it difficult to keep going when the way gets hard, is lacking Christian maturity and perseverance.

Slippery When Wet

It's always a good idea to slow down when it starts raining, because it takes longer to stop on a wet pavement than a dry one. What many drivers do not know is that a street may be more slippery as the result of a light shower than from a downpour. Why? Streets and highways collect little particles of dust and oil. When mixed with just a little water, the surface becomes dangerously slippery. But after a downpour, much of the oil is washed away.

There's another kind of "wetness" on the highway. By that, we do not mean rainfall, but alcoholic beverages which some drivers drink. A drinking driver finds that his reactions are "slippery," i.e., he cannot think and react as fast. This may result not only in death or injury for himself, but for those in other cars, too. More often than not, the driver who has had just one or two drinks is more dangerous than the fully intoxicated person. If a fellow is drunk, he can hardly operate a car to begin with; but just a few drinks may make him overconfident and reckless.

Drinking not only harms a person while he is driving, but

makes him less efficient whatever he is doing. Rain on the street is dangerous. Liquor in the man is dangerous, too!

Hymns: "I'll Go Where You Want Me to Go"
          "O Master, Let Me Walk With Thee"

Prayer: Our Father, make us alert to the signs along life's highway. Help us to understand that they are for our benefit and safety. Bring each of us to a safe destination, not only on the streets and highways, but also in our personal lives. Amen.

3 Play Ball!

Preparation: This program is built around five games or sports, each of which uses a ball and some device to strike the ball. You will need a baseball bat, tennis racket, croquet mallet, Ping-Pong paddle, and a golf club. If you wish, you may bring the balls that go with these sports, but the emphasis is on the objects used to strike the balls. A key word is used to describe each of the five bats or clubs. In nearly every instance, however, the key words are interchangeable. Feel free to select other key words if they seem to illustrate the purpose better.

Baseball Bat

Here is a game that all of us have played at one time or another. Baseball has been called the all-American pastime. During the World Series each fall, life almost comes to a standstill in cities and towns across the nation as millions listen and watch on television. Who can show us the proper way to hold this bat? And when a batter steps up to the mound, what is his objective? Yes, he wants to knock a home

10

run, a line drive that will see him safely around the bases.

The key word, then, is "drive." Otherwise, the batter strikes out or hits a foul. In many ways, you and I come up to bat every day of our lives. Oh, not out there on the diamond, but in the choices we make, the jobs we have to perform, the opportunities we face. We can be a hard-hitter for what is right and decent, or we can hit a foul or strike out. When you read Ecclesiastes 9:10, think of it as a challenge to knock a home run every time you have a chance: "Whatsoever thy hand findeth to do, do it with thy might."

Tennis Racket

Do you remember what happened the first time you tried to play tennis? You probably held the racket underhand, and when you hit the ball it went way up in the air and outside the court. A tennis racket is not designed to drive the ball a long distance, but to return the ball to the proper section of the court on the other side of the net.

"Accuracy" might be the key word. Regardless of how much force one uses to strike the ball with the racket, his main objective is to serve or return the ball with accuracy.

The more complex life becomes, the greater the need for accuracy. Think of accuracy in filling a prescription, in landing an airliner, in timing a television program, or in cashing a check. Accuracy is essential in one's personal life, too. Are we accurate in what we say about others, or in how we quote others? Are we accurate (honest) in the promises we make, the responsibilities we assume? The careless life is the scoreless life.

Croquet Mallet

When you play tennis or baseball, you must make a quick decision in returning the ball. Not so in croquet. You can walk all around the ball, get down on all fours, measure the distance to the wicket, or "sight" the direction you wish the ball to go. Then it is important that you hit the wooden ball with a solid, even stroke of the mallet. Distance is sometimes a factor, but more often the definiteness or evenness with which you hit the ball is what counts. "Prejudgment" is the key word! Slowly and deliberately if necessary, one predetermines exactly where he wants the ball to roll. Then he strikes the ball, not so much with force as with a show of solidity and strength—measured strength, that is.

All of us have seen the person who seems to be going in all directions at once. He may be going like a house afire, making a big noise, but he never seems to accomplish much. Is it possible his life lacks direction and purpose, strength and solidarity? A skilled croquet player hits the balls with a solid whack. The same principle applies in the game of life.

Ping-Pong Paddle

Let's use "bounce" as the key word in Ping-Pong. Note how the ball bounces as it is driven first to one side of the net, then to the other. Even when it falls off the table, it continues bouncing.

Ping-Pong certainly demands accuracy and aim. But the paddle is used basically to bounce the ball back to the other player. Ping-Pong players do not make line drives or home runs. They keep the ball bouncing!

When we go through periods of depression or discouragement, we feel pretty low. Someone says, "Snap out of it!" But it's not always that easy, is it? Yet we admire the person who has the resilience that enables him to bounce back from difficulties. This is a trait that can be learned, if we wish. But we must want to. Unfortunately, some people seem to enjoy feeling low or blue.

Try thinking of yourself as a Ping-Pong ball. Determine to spend less time in self-pity. When you fail, analyze the reason why. Then make a comeback. Try again. Bounce back. Don't get discouraged. When you fall, get up. When you slip, get up. Get up—bounce back—try again. No one can fail all the time!

Golf Club

If you have played any golf, you know that you select a club on the basis of the distance you want to drive the ball. If you are on the green, you pick the putter for a drive of a few feet. If you are teeing off, you may select a wood to drive the ball several hundred feet.

In golf, let's think of "distance" as the key word.

How far do you want to go in life? You say it doesn't matter how you feel about it? That's where you're wrong! Very few people go farther than they plan. The distance depends on the dream! There are very few things that the human mind is capable of visualizing that cannot be achieved.

In the novel *Spencer's Mountain,* a teen-ager dreams of being the first from his mountain family to go to college. He faces many difficulties. But one day his family stands by the highway and watches him board a Greyhound bus for a college town. As the teen-ager finds a seat at the rear, another passenger asks a question: "You going far, boy?"'

"Yes, real far," the boy answered!

Hymns: "Higher Ground"
"Dare to Be Brave, Dare to Be True"

Prayer: Our Father, we thank thee for leisure time, for sports and games and friends. We thank thee for the pleasure and relaxation they afford, and the skill they demand in us. Help us to be conscientious in the great game of life, to obey the rules, to score as high as possible, and to be good sports when we fail. We pray in the name of Christ, who came that we might have life, and have it more abundantly. Amen.

4 A Tool for Every Job

Preparation: If you do not have the tools suggested, perhaps you can borrow them. Or you may wish to design your own program built around other tools. There are so many tools that you will be limited only by your own imagination. (In addition to those mentioned here, you might use a hammer, tape rule, pliers, wrench, chisel, square, transit, bit and brace, claw hammer, mallet, file, or others.) A bricklayer, carpenter, or mechanic might be enlisted to help in your presentation. You might bring extra tools for display, in addition to the four or five you use for object lessons.

Saw

A saw is one of the commonest of tools. Most often, it is used to cut a piece of wood or other building material to fit into a particular place. Seldom does a piece of lumber come in the exact size or length. The raw lumber must be sawed into a number of lengths to make a building. Our jobs, our lives, our families, our churches—all of these are more complex than a hundred-story building. The pieces must be fitted and cut. This is an endless task—it goes on day after day as long as we live. No one ever gets his life "just right." We must be adaptable to change, and willing to cut (give in) here and there. This may mean slicing a dream in half to achieve what is best for one's family. It may mean adjusting one's desires or schedules to what is best for serving his church.

Plane

The sharp, cutting edge of a plane is used to smooth a rough surface. It acts something like sandpaper. When I see someone using a plane, I think of the seventh Beatitude, "Blessed are the peacemakers: for they shall be called the children of God" (Matt. 5:9). I also think of the prophecy of Christ, "Every valley shall be filled, and every mountain and hill shall be brought low; and the crooked shall be made straight, and the rough ways shall be made smooth" (Luke 3:5).

No one will deny that there are many rough spots in life which need smoothing. Think of the rough, unconquered diseases. Think of the rough, destructive power of war. Think of the roughness of hate, suspicion, jealousy, and fear. Think of the roughness of unforgiven sin, of broken homes, of one-parent children.

All of us can pray for grace to serve as a smoothing effect on friends and families and conditions about us. Rather than promoting discord and encouraging disharmony, we can be used to smooth out the rough places, to fill in the valleys, and to level the hills.

Level

Have you ever watched a bricklayer as he used the level to get his rows of bricks perfectly straight? Or a carpenter, as he used the level to line up a door or window? A level does just what it says—it levels a wall or a door, both perpendicular and horizontal. The level and the plane are similar.

We sometimes say, "Why don't you 'level' with me?" By that, we mean we want the truth. We want the facts as they are. We detest hypocrisy and half-truths. "Are you on the level with me?" is a question we use to test the friendship of others.

Evasiveness, hypocrisy, and deception are signs of character weakness. We resent these factors in others; others resent the same in us. We may do little about helping others to live and talk on the "level," but we can make sure that our own lives are characterized by straightforwardness and truthfulness.

Screwdriver

A screwdriver is used either to tighten or loosen a screw. You can't drive a screw into a board, nor yank it out with a claw hammer. It must be turned to be effective. Note that a screwdriver is very adaptable—it will turn either to the right or to the left. It is just as effective in either direction.

It has been said that a wise man changes his mind, but that a fool never does. The person with a changeless mind turns the screwdriver in the same direction all the time. We might say that he is a fool.

Certainly, there are some basic convictions about life

which are as changeless as God himself. But on the other hand, there are many attitudes and customs and opinions that should be changed—not only once in a lifetime, but maybe many times. Take, for example, our attitude toward our friends. We form an opinion which later proves to be wrong. It may be that we have been patterning our behavior after some facet of a friend's personality which proves to be less than admirable. Or we may find that some weakness in a friend turns out to be a strength. Adaptability means that we are willing to admit our errors and change our attitudes and opinions toward other people.

We may need to be adaptable in our attitude toward God, also. Take prayer, for example. A child may have a very immature, Santa Claus idea of how God answers prayer. As the child grows up, he finds this attitude is wrong. Can his concepts of God stand to be changed, or does he hold relentlessly to the ideas of his childhood?

Trowel

A bricklayer uses the trowel to smooth the mortar and spread it evenly. If mortar is left in the big batches in which it is made, it hardens into a useless mass. Only as it is spread thinly and evenly does it achieve usefulness.

Your life and mine are filled with many wonderful blessings, which can be used to benefit the lives of other people. But they must be spread out. If we don't share them, our lives harden and grow cold. But if spread out, these blessings serve as living mortar to fuse and bind the best that is in others.

Don't allow yourself to harden into a cold lump of indifference. Remember the trowel. Extend yourself to the world about you.

Hymns: "Building, Daily Building" (*Songs for Juniors*)
          "Make Me a Channel of Blessing"

Prayer: We praise thee, our Father, for skilled hands that take raw materials and ingenious tools and use them to build and create. Likewise, may we be creative and constructive in all we do, using the tools of friendliness and unselfishness to bless all with whom we come in contact. Amen.

5 Dressed for Action

Preparation: This program centers on articles of clothing, either men's, women's, or children's. You may simply display the different items, or have four or five persons model them. For the helmet, use one worn by construction workers or by military personnel. Select a coat with bright, rather gaudy colors. A brightly striped sport coat would be good.

Shoes

In Bible times, many of the people went barefoot, or else wore sandles which consisted mainly of a sole fastened to the foot with cords. This is why the Bible often mentions the washing of feet—it was a sign of hospitality to offer a basin of water to a visitor whose feet might be tired from a journey.

Think of the variety of shoes in today's department stores —dress, leisure, work, military, and others. There is even greater variety in the styles of dress shoes, particularly for women. But of more importance than the kind of shoes we wear is where our feet take us. Isaiah 52:7 says, "How beautiful upon the mountains are the feet of him that bringeth good tidings, that publisheth peace." Bad news travels fast, but good news is always welcome in any household. When someone sees us coming, do they say, "Here is a chance to hear the latest gossip" ? Or do they say, "Oh, I am so glad to see you, for you always have something nice to say." Even if we must go barefoot here in the twentieth century, let our feet take us on errands of goodwill and kindness.

Helmet

Helmets are frequently worn by construction workers, firemen, policemen, and soldiers. In Bible times, rather ornate, heavy helmets were worn by the military. Ephesians 6:13–17 describes the uniform or armor to be worn by the Christian soldier who engages in spiritual warfare. "The helmet of salvation" (v. 17) is suggested for the head.

In what sense is salvation a "helmet" ? Consider the purpose of a helmet—protection. What is the supreme protection God gives to us through Christ? It is salvation. Sometimes we call this being converted or being saved or being born again. Salvation comes when we are truly sorry for our sins, ask God's forgiveness, and put our faith in Christ alone instead of any good thing we may have done.

A steel worker wouldn't do construction work on a skyscraper without a helmet. A sensible person will not face the temptations and difficulties of everyday life without the helmet of God's salvation.

Coat

One of the most interesting Bible stories having to do with clothing is that of Joseph's coat of many colors, given to him by his father Jacob. But the coat proved to be a curse instead of a blessing. His eleven brothers were jealous. They resented the favoritism Joseph received. They also resented the dreams he described to them, in which he seemed to be destined for a place of authority. As a result, the brothers sold Joseph into slavery in Egypt. (If you wish to tell more details of the story, see the thirty-seventh chapter of Genesis.)

When we remember his bright coat, let it be a reminder to us never to show favoritism. Playing favorites disrupts homes, separates friends, and arouses suspicion on the job.

Topcoat

Jesus taught that a person should go to all reasonable ends to avoid misunderstandings and hard feelings. So in Matthew 5:40 he said, "If any man will sue thee at the law, and take away thy coat, let him have thy cloak also." To avoid conflict, Jesus suggested that a man give away his topcoat (cloak) as well as his coat. In other words, the Christian is to do more than is expected.

This is not a bad rule for every area of life. Imagine children who do more than is expected around the house. Imagine an employee who works harder than expected. Think of a student who consistently does more than is assigned. Visualize a person of talent and ability who gives far more of himself to society than is demanded. Think of a conscientious steward who gives more of his money than is asked. Imagine a husband or wife who give more of their love than the ordinary marriage demands. The next time you put on a topcoat, think not only of how it will keep you warm, but visualize it as a symbol of the motto, "Do more than is expected!"

Skirt

Psalm 133 has only three verses. It describes how the oil that was used to anoint Aaron as a priest ran down on his beard and then to his skirts. (In Old Testament times, the priestly garments included a "skirt.") The oil was intended only for his head, but evidently so much was poured on that it ran down his whole body.

Psalm 133 teaches that just as the ointment covered Aaron, so a spirit of friendliness and fellowship should cover those who love God. "Behold, how good and how pleasant it is for brethren to dwell together in unity!" (v. 1).

Just as a skirt completely encircles the waist, so should unity and understanding encircle the people of God. This does not mean that we who are men should start wearing skirts! It does mean that the Christian is not fully dressed until he shows a spirit of fellowship and peace. The bickering Christian who can get along with no one is hardly dressed!

Hymns: "Footsteps of Jesus"
"Rise Up, O Men of God"

Prayer: Clothe us, O God, with thy righteousness. Hide our nakedness of sin and disobedience. Crown us with thy salvation, and put on our feet the sandles of good news. Make us generous and glad, and save us from the narrowness and provincialism of favoritism. In the name of our Saviour. Amen.

6 Deliver That Package!

Preparation: Wrap five boxes of various sizes with heavy brown paper, as if for mailing. To each box, stick one of the labels described below. If you cannot secure printed labels, write the message on the wrapping paper in bold letters. Your post office may have some of these labels. Or if you know someone who works in the shipping department of a mail-order house or wholesale company, he may give you some. Arrange the boxes where all can read the labels. Or, you may hold up each one in turn. Better still, enlist five "messengers" who appear before your group with their box at the appropriate time.

"Do Not Open Until Christmas"

Here is a label we see all through December. It spells excitement and curiosity and surprise. Christmas, birthday, or other gifts are more fun if we wait for the big event to open them. If we slip around and peek, we not only spoil the fun for ourselves but for those who make the gift. Most things in life are that way. There is a right time and a wrong time.

24

As Ecclesiastes 3:1 says, "To every thing there is a season, and a time to every purpose under the heaven."

A fifteen-year-old thinks he *must* drive. The law in most states says he must wait until sixteen, and some states insist on eighteen. Now there is no sin in driving a car. But there is a time to drive, and that is when the one reaches the legal age and meets the other qualifications. If one jumps the gun, opens the package before Christmas, violates the driver-licensing laws—he spoils the fun for others as well as himself.

Sex is another area. Christians believe that intimate sex relations are for two persons whose love for each other has been solemnized by marriage. But some think that sex is to be enjoyed as soon as one reaches physical maturity, without recognizing that emotional and spiritual maturity are often longer in coming. Yet these are more important than mere physical maturity in true sexual fulfilment.

Perhaps you can think of other choices which are marred, because of the impatience that leads one to break open the package too soon.

"Special Delivery—Rush"

Special delivery says, "Do this first. The other packages can be delivered later." Most of what we do in life is important. But some matters are more important. Some demand prime attention and priority. Let's look at three.

One should give top priority to deciding on Christ as the master of his life. Some put this off, thinking that they can wait to become Christians until death is near. But Christ came to give us abundant life here on earth, as well as eternal life in the world to come. If we are looking for a verse of Scripture that suggests the idea of urgency, we can find no better than Joshua 24:15, "Choose you this day whom ye will serve."

Special attention should be given to deciding on and preparing for one's life vocation. Too many stumble into one job, and then as quickly stumble out. Each of us has only one life, and that life is too valuable to waste on jumping from one job to another. We should decide on a vocation —as early as possible—and then make whatever preparation is necessary. This may mean college, a trade school, vocational training, or graduate school. But whatever it takes, do it now. *Special delivery*, that is!

Prime attention should also be given to deciding on a wife or husband, one's lifetime mate. Again, too many young people stumble and fumble into marriage. They confuse love with physical attraction for the opposite sex. Love includes sex, but it also includes more. By using "special delivery" for marriage, we do not mean that one should rush into marriage with all possible speed. We do mean that one should give his best thinking, praying, and studying to the selection of a mate. Other "packages" can wait.

"Perishable"

If you don't deliver this package today, there will be no need to do so tomorrow. It will be worthless, its contents probably spoiled or melted. We think of Jeremiah 8:20, "The harvest is past, the summer is ended, and we are not saved."

Four things cannot be called back—the spent bullet, the spoken word, the missed opportunity, and yesterday.

There is one real sense in which death is a blessing: it is a constant reminder that we do not have forever to achieve our goals. Each tick of the watch and each turn of the calendar tells us that yesterday is gone, tomorrow is only a dream, and all we have is today.

Grab for dear life those opportunities that come your way. Hold on to them. Exploit them. Use them. Put your talents to work on them. Don't let them rot in your hands, for they are perishable, you know!

"Handle with Care—Fragile"

Let's imagine this box contains delicate chinaware or sensitive instruments. To drop it on the floor is to ruin the contents. So we obey the warning, "Do not drop."

In a sense, friendships are fragile. Yet we often take them for granted. Friendship, like a garden, needs attention. Otherwise it will be choked with weeds of indifference and die of neglect.

The promises we make are very fragile. It takes so little effort to drop and break a promise. All that is required is just to "forget" that we made it. Once we make a promise, let's clutch it tightly until it is fulfilled, whether the promise is to a friend, a relative, or to God.

Christian consecration, because it is largely a promise, is easily broken and marred. We make great resolutions, determine to lead a consecrated life, and then break only one small vow. But that one vow can start a chain reaction that drops the package of consecration to the floor, where it shatters into pieces.

"This End Up"

Knowing which end of a parcel is "up" is like knowing what things in life are important. Does life ever seem crazy and mixed-up to you? Is it possible you are majoring on minors, and minoring on majors? Are you standing on your head, instead of having both feet firmly planted on the ground?

Sometimes we feel that life is like a furniture store which is broken into one night. The culprit doesn't steal anything —he merely switches the price tags! The next morning, a $400 television is tagged for $1.25, and a $1.25 whisk broom is tagged for $400. This is getting the top on the bottom, and the bottom on top.

Chaos is the inevitable result, whether in a furniture store or a person's life. Good judgment is the key. Sometimes we call this common sense. But call it what you will, unless one knows which end of life is "up," he finds himself in a crazy, mixed-up world.

Hymns: "Work, for the Night Is Coming"
            "I Surrender All"

Prayer: Help us, O God, to read clearly the labels of life.
            Help us to "deliver the goods" on time and in good
            condition. Amen.

7 Color It Red

Preparation: Colors are used in this program as attention-getters. You may illustrate these colors in a number of ways. Perhaps the most dramatic way is to secure four large balloons. Each would be a different color. Some department and five-and-ten stores will inflate their balloons with helium, at slightly extra cost. This makes them float. Attach long strings to them and anchor them to some object at the front of your room or auditorium. Let them float almost to the ceiling. These will attract attention the very minute your audience walks in. Point to the balloons in turn as you discuss the color involved.

Truly, ours is a wonderful world of color. In addition to the color in nature—clouds and sky, seas and lakes, flowers and birds, sunsets and snowstorms—we find color used lavishly in modern clothing, decorating, furniture, cars, magazines, movies, and television. Color is what the eye sees when light strikes it: apples reflect red light, grass reflects green, and so on. The human eye can see a million or more different colors. Color affects our emotions, and it can help make us tired or refreshed, sad or happy, ill at ease or comfortable. We use warm shades in the living areas of our homes, as they suggest sociability. Cool shades have a quieting effect for study and sleeping. Bright, circus colors relieve monotony and make a kitchen cheerful. A hospital patient making normal recovery may do better in a room with warm colors like pink, peach, and ivory, for these are cheerful colors which help him want to get well. If he faces a long convalescence, a room that is soft green, blue-green, or gray may help him feel relaxed and comfortable. These are the cool colors.

Red

Look at the red balloon. Red is one of the most popular colors on the spectrum. We use the word daily in our conversation. Public documents used to be tied with red cloth, so we blame useless delays on red tape. If we get behind with our bills, we are in the red. Red is the color of the badge of courage, and Julia Ward Howe once wrote a poem, "The Flag," in which she made the two synonymous. In our American flag, she saw some stripes "red with the blood of freemen" while others were "white with the fear of the foe." A ruddy complexion usually indicates good health, whereas we identify illness and even death with the paleness of human flesh drained of blood. We observe the Lord's Supper with the cup of grape juice, a reminder that Christ gave his very lifeblood for us.

Red challenges us to be loyal, constant, courageous, and sacrificial.

Green

The green balloon reminds us of envy, which Shakespeare in *Antony and Cleopatra* described as the "green sickness." And in *Othello*, he wrote:

> O, beware, my lord, of jealousy;
> It is the green-eyed monster which doth mock
> The meat it feeds on.

We also associate green with sourness, "That apple is as green as a persimmon."

On the other hand, green suggests tranquility and quiet. Cecil F. Alexander suggests this idea in her hymn about the crucifixion, and somehow the way in which she says it seems to soften the impact of Christ's death:

> There is a green hill far away,
> Without a city wall,
> Where the dear Lord was crucified,
> Who died to save us all.

Rather than limiting the meaning of green to envy, we should let this color remind us that life needs a softening and quieting influence.

Yellow

Yellow has long been associated with cowardice or fear. We say a traitor or coward or someone who backs down at the last minute is "yellow." And although silence is often golden, it can also be yellow. Yellow is the last color most of us would prefer to be labeled. We agree with J. J. Walker that the "blues of mental and physical wear are not as devastating as the yellows of the quitter."

When we look at Calvary, we think of the color yellow reflected in the treachery and cowardice of Judas Iscariot. Greedy for yellow gold, he played the yellow role in betraying our Lord.

Yellow makes a pretty balloon—it never makes a pretty person!

Blue

To some persons, blue is depressing. "Here it is blue Monday again." "I've got the blues." Or we sing, "It'll Be a Blue Christmas Without You," or listen plaintively to the "St. Louis Blues."

To others, blue is a soft, delicate color. We think of the sky-blue color of bird eggs in the spring. We say a person's eyes are as blue as the sky. Blue is the color of truth and loyalty and integrity. We compliment a person for his honesty and faithfulness by saying he is "true-blue." The stars of our flags are on a blue background. Blue is a patriotic color that inspires loyalty and service to one's country.

The Christian strives to be "true-blue" to his Lord, to his country, to his church, to his friends, to his family, and, of course, to himself.

(You may think of character traits identified with other colors, and find balloons of corresponding shades.)

Hymns: "For the Beauty of the Earth"
            "Though Your Sins Be As Scarlet"

Prayer: We praise thee, O God, for thy creative power
which has taken the colors of the rainbow and
scattered them over the face of the earth and sky.
We thank thee for sight, that enables us to drink
up the visual beauty about us. Help us not to mar
thy creation, nor to mix the colors in hideous re-
bellion. May our lives reflect the beauty of thy
universe, and may our everyday deeds mirror the
radiance of the rainbow. Amen.

8 The Other Six Days

Preparation: Serving God through one's vocation is the theme of this devotional. If used with children or young people, it should be slanted to vocational choice. If with adults, the emphasis will be more on making the most of one's vocation as a way of glorifying God. The plan is for four or five persons, dressed in their distinguishing uniforms, to describe their work. Several extras are suggested, so you can choose four or five from the ones that may be available in your community. It will be more effective to use persons actually serving in these professions. If this is not possible, borrow their uniforms and let someone else act the part. (The attorney may wear a robe.)

Note this is not a program in which you do the talking, but one in which each person describes his career in his own words. These are not to be memorized speeches. The material below is suggestive only. Each person should devise his own three-minute presentation.

You might start by reading this poem by Edgar Frank:

A man I know has made an altar
Of his factory bench,
And one has turned the counter in his store
Into a place of sacrifice and holy ministry.

Another still has changed his office-desk
Into a pulpit-desk, from which to speak and write,
Transforming commonplace affairs
Into the business of the King.

A Martha in our midst has made
Her kitchen-table a communion-table,
A postman makes his daily round
A walk in the temple of God.

To all of these each daily happening
Has come to be a whisper from the lips of God,
Each separate task a listening-post,
And every common circumstance
A wayside shrine.

Fireman

My job is to be on duty when needed. That may be at two
o'clock in the morning. It might be on Christmas Day or the
Fourth of July. But whenever fire and danger strike, I am
ready to respond within a few short minutes. My job is to
serve and protect, to save lives and preserve property. Because I am on duty, others can sleep peacefully, knowing
that men and equipment are ready if danger strikes. In my
work, I try to witness for Christ by . . .

Stewardess

I do everything from fluffing a pillow for a seventy-eight-
year-old grandmother to warming the formula for a baby

on its first flight. My responsibility is to provide for the comfort of the passengers who make up my flights. Although there is little time to spend with any one passenger, I try to be pleasant and helpful to everyone I meet. On my flights, I try to witness for Christ by . . .

Barber or Beautician

All kinds of people come through my shop each week. Although my work is concerned with their personal grooming and appearance, I also find opportunities to talk as well as listen to those I meet. I find the following doors are open for witnessing for Christ . . .

Auto Mechanic

When a customer drives his car into my garage, I feel that my first responsibility is an honest, thorough repair job for him. But I notice that the people who bring their cars for repairs often are in need of "fixing" themselves! I try to be alert for witnessing opportunities, and here are some I have discovered . . .

Soldier, Sailor, or Marine

My job is the defense of our nation. Today, young men in military service go all over the world on tours of duty. We make many new friends from our own country as well as around the world. I am trained to dress neatly and to give a good impression of our nation. As a Christian, I feel I should also be a good soldier for Jesus Christ, and make a good impression for him. I try to witness by . . .

Postman

Perhaps you have read the slogan of the U.S. Post Office Department, engraved on the front of the New York City General Post Office: "Neither snow nor rain nor heat nor gloom of night stays these couriers from the swift completion of their appointed rounds." This slogan reminds us that we are to deliver the mail, whatever happens. Most of us have a keen sense of our responsibility to maintain communication through the printed word, as we deliver letters, newspapers, magazines, and business mail. My work brings me in contact with many people, and I try to witness by . . .

Attorney

The people I serve are usually in some kind of trouble. Their difficulties may be financial, marital, or criminal. My job is not to see that the guilty escape punishment, but to help insure that every person receives the justice that is due him under the law. Although I cannot go into a courtroom and preach a sermon to the jury, I am able to witness for Christ by . . .

Policeman

Like the fireman, I work to protect the people. Whereas he protects them from fire, I protect them from traffic hazards, mob violence, and lawbreakers. I meet a lot of people we ordinarily classify as undesirables. But no person is undesirable to Christ. He sees potential good in everyone. For this reason, I try to witness to everyone, regardless of how hardened he may be. Some of my opportunities are . . .

Doctor, Nurse, or Medical Technician

My job is not only to help people get well, but to practice preventive medicine so that they will not get sick. Jesus is called the Great Physician, because he was concerned with people's bodies as well as their souls. Often a sick person is a disagreeable person. He doesn't feel well, and illness may bring out his worst side. Frequently, the patient has other emotional and spiritual problems which are the real causes of his physical illness. His loved ones are often tense and worried. I watch for opportunities to witness to patients and their families. Here is how I do it . . .

Hymns: "Work, for the Night Is Coming"
            "To the Work"

Prayer: Our Father, we thank thee for all the skills and talents with which you have blessed mankind. We thank thee for the farmer that produces our food, for those who serve in industry to provide cars and furniture and tools, and for all those in the service ministries who meet our personal needs. May we look upon each vocation as an avenue for service. May every home, workbench, and place of business be a pulpit and an altar place where men are pointed to Christ, the Lamb of God, who takes away the sin of the world. In his name. Amen.

9 More Than Bread

Preparation: Items of food are used in this program to show how the Bible illustrates basic spiritual truths with food. The truth is that man has far deeper needs than merely satisfying his physical hunger.

Since the object lessons are rather small, this program may be more effective with smaller groups, say up to fifty.

This could be an ideal program for use near Thanksgiving.

Saltshaker

This little shaker I am holding can be found in almost every kitchen and on every restaurant table. Salt is very plentiful. It is found beneath the ground in almost all parts of the world. And if the oceans should dry up, they would leave enough salt to cover almost the entire United States with a layer more than a mile and a half deep!

But salt was not always so plentiful. In the days of the Roman Empire, it was so scarce that Caesar's soldiers received part of their pay in salt. It was known as their *salarium,* from which we get our word "salary." So, if a person is doing a good job, we say he is earning his salt!

Among other things, salt preserves and flavors. In these days of deepfreezes and quick refrigeration, salt is not nearly so important as a preservative as it was in Jesus' day. But when Jesus said, "Ye are the salt of the earth" (Matt. 5:13), his hearers grasped the idea that just as salt would keep their food from spoiling and rotting, so Christians should help preserve society from rotting.

And who can enjoy good food without the flavor and sparkle that salt adds? Persons on salt-free diets can tell you how tasteless food is without seasoning. Now if we are the salt of the earth, this means we bring joy and flavor to life. Life without Christ is dull, insipid, and meaningless. Only the Christian faith can bring flavor to an otherwise flat life.

Loaf of Bread

Many people feel that a meal is incomplete without some kind of bread—whether it be rolls, sliced bread, corn bread, biscuits, or what have you! Jesus said, "I am the bread of life: he that cometh to me shall never hunger" (John 6:35). Christ, then, is the staff of our lives, and as indispensable as bread on the table.

After we enjoy a meal of hot rolls, meat, and potatoes, we find ourselves hungry again in a few hours. Yet Jesus claimed that the spiritual bread he offers can quench one's hunger forever.

Does this mean that when one becomes a Christian he receives such a blessing that he never hungers or thirsts for spiritual food again? No, because all of us need to grow daily in grace and Christian maturity. It does mean, however, that faith in Christ brings a lasting, permanent satisfaction. Our faith is not a temporary emotion that is here today and gone tomorrow. Once Christ enters our life, he is an enduring source of strength—not only for this life, but for all eternity.

Canned Fish (*Tuna, Salmon, etc.*)

John 6:5–14 describes how Jesus fed five thousand people with a little boy's lunch, which consisted of only five pieces of bread and two fishes. When we serve fish in our homes, it can be a reminder of the unselfishness of the lad who was willing to give what he had. No one remembers his name, but millions through the centuries have read of his unselfishness with fond admiration. Fish can also remind us of the miraculous powers of Christ, who was able to feed so many with so little. Fish can be a symbol of how God takes the little we have and, if it is dedicated to him, greatly multiplies it.

The question is not how many "fish" we have in our lunch, but our willingness to use what we have for God's glory and for the service of others.

The fish was a secret symbol used by the early Christians during the times of persecution to keep their identity secret from the Roman officials. This symbol has been found by excavators in first-century Pompeii and in the catacombs along Rome's Appian and Ostian Ways. Why was a fish used? Perhaps because the five letters of the Greek word for fish are the initials (or first letters) of the five words "Jesus

Christ, Son (of) God, Saviour." These five letters made a sacred acrostic for the early Christians. (For more information, look up the word "symbol" in a Bible dictionary or encyclopedia.)

Grapes

Grapes are mentioned prominently throughout the Bible. Remember that when Moses sent twelve men to spy out the Promised Land, they found one bunch of grapes so large that it took two men to carry it, suspended upon a pole (Num. 13:23).

One of the best known proverbs of the Bible is found in Ezekiel 18:2, "The fathers have eaten sour grapes, and the children's teeth are set on edge." Have you ever eaten a sour grape and your teeth felt gritty? The point of this proverb is that children sometimes suffer for the misdeeds (sour grapes) of their parents. This does not mean that God holds children responsible for what their fathers or mothers do, or that he takes out his wrath on them. It simply means that each succeeding generation is affected to some degree by the preceding generation. For example, mothers that experiment with LSD may give birth to deformed children. Or the deformity might even show up in their grandchildren or great-grandchildren!

A good policy is to eat grapes that are ripe. They taste better, anyway!

Bottle or Can of Milk and Jar of Honey

Milk and honey are synonymous in the Bible with peace, prosperity, and plenty. Milk was an important part of the diet in Bible times—not only the milk of cows, but also of sheep, camels, and goats. Goat milk was highly esteemed, although few of us would agree today!

When the Jewish people were in exile in Egypt, God promised that he would bring them to Canaan, a land "flowing with milk and honey" (Ex. 3:8).

Later, God warned them against pride and ingratitude when they came into Canaan and enjoyed "houses full of all good things, which thou filledst not, and wells digged, which thou diggedst not, vineyards and olive trees, which thou plantedst not; when thou shalt have eaten and be full" (Deut. 6:11).

When we are discouraged, afraid, hungry, poor, or sick, it is easy to call on God. But when the sun is shining, and we enjoy prosperity and good health, and our tables are filled with milk and honey, it is easy to forget God. It is easy to credit ourselves for all the blessings of life, for all the material things we feel we have worked so hard to earn.

The next time we drink a glass of milk or spread honey on a hot biscuit, let's take time to breathe a prayer of thanks to God, the source of every good and perfect gift (James 1:17).

Apple

If there is time (or if you wish to substitute for one of the above items), use an apple, basing your application on Proverbs 25:11: "A word fitly spoken is like apples of gold in pictures of silver." Or, look in a concordance for Bible references to other foods. You may find enough ideas for two or three programs.

Hymns: "Break Thou the Bread of Life"
"Jesus Is All the World to Me"

Prayer: O God, thou art all in all. Without thee, we are nothing. We hunger and thirst for thee. We are grateful for the bounties of the fields that bring abundance to our tables. But more than this, we want thee. Satisfy us with good things, so that our strength is renewed like the eagle's. Save us from pride and ingratitude, and fill us with thanksgiving. Amen.

10 The Shoes of Happiness

Preparation: Think of the infinite variety of shoes in the world! Work shoes and play shoes; high-topped boots and low-cut sandals; shoes with laces and shoes with zippers; black shoes, white shoes, and all the colors of the rainbow in between; soldiers' boots that slosh through the mud or snow, and babies' shoes preserved in bronze.

> Tip at the toe, live to see woe;
> Wear at the side, live to be a bride;
> Wear at the ball, live to spend all;
> Wear at the heel, live to save a deal.[1]

The attention-getters for this devotional are several pairs of shoes. Choose a variety of them, matching them as best you can to your story.

This program is based on the poem "The Shoes of Happiness," by Edwin Markham. For background information,

---

[1] Anonymous, "The Wear of Old Shoes," *The Home Book of Quotations,* ed. Burton Stevenson (New York: Dodd, Mead, and Co., 1934), p. 1817.

try to locate this poem and read it in its entirety.[2] *You will find it in part on pages 25 through 33 of William L. Stidger's* There Are Sermons in Books.[3]

This morning (or tonight) I want to tell you about an Oriental sultan who lived many years ago. Like all of us, he wanted happiness. But he was ill and discouraged, and had almost given up. Finally, someone suggested to him, "Find a happy person, and wear his shoes." So he called a servant and sent him out to find a truly happy man. If the servant found one, he was to bring that man's shoes to the sultan. He would put them on and find happiness!

Where do you think the servant turned first? You're right! He talked to a rich man, because like most of us he thought that riches bring happiness. He looked at the shoes the rich man was wearing, and here is what they looked like. (Hold up your first attention-getter—a pair of expensive-looking shoes.) But the rich man excused himself, "I am sorry, my riches have not made me glad."

Surprised, but not discouraged, the servant turned to a poor man. Here are the shoes he was wearing (hold up a pair of worn-out shoes). But the poor man said he worried too much about feeding his children to be joyful.

Next, he turned to an aged person. Here are the shoes he was wearing (hold up a pair of old-fashioned shoes). But the old man was too sad thinking about the past to be glad.

---

[2] Originally published in Markham's *The Shoes of Happiness, and Other Poems* (New York: Doubleday, Page and Co., 1915).
[3] (Nashville: Abingdon Press, 1922).

Then the servant talked to a young person, who was wearing these shoes (a pair of new, stylish shoes). But he was too restless for tomorrow to enjoy today.

He talked to a soldier who was wearing these combat boots. Surely the soldier, who had just returned in a bright uniform to a hero's welcome, would be joyous. But the soldier's eyes filled with tears as he remembered "comrades left on the battle hill."

In desperation the servant sought out a wise man, a scholar, who was wearing these shoes (black dress shoes). But the man of wisdom said, "I am not glad; I am only wise."

With this, the servant gave up and started home. He dreaded to report to the sultan. On the way, he heard "a fluting sound from a field of corn." Turning aside to see who was playing, he found a fellow stretched out on the ground, using his arm for a pillow and blowing "thin, sweet sounds from a pipe of willow." Here at last was a happy man. The servant begged for his shoes so that the sultan might wear them. "But you see," answered the joyous one, "I have no shoes."

When Jesus sent the disciples on a mission, he advised them to "Provide neither gold, nor silver, . . . nor scrip for your journey, neither two coats, neither shoes" (Matt. 10:9–10).

I think we all get the point: shoes, cars, money, television, steaks, and jewelry can add to the enjoyment of life—but material things do not guarantee happiness. The happiest people around us may be those who have found joy in the little things of life, even though their feet are bare and their heads are hatless.

Hymns: "More Love to Thee, O Christ"
            "I've Found a Friend, oh, Such a Friend"

Prayer: Gracious Father, we are grateful for the material
            blessings of life. But forgive us when we confuse
            tangible things with the intangible joys. Fill us
            with love and friendship for thee and others. May
            we look for true happiness by putting a song in the
            hearts of others, rather than always seeking music
            for our own ears. Amen.

11 Let's Ride Bikes!

Preparation: Children's toys, such as wagons, tricycles, and sleds, are suggested for this program. If you have a small meeting place, you may wonder how you will have room for these toys, especially the bigger ones. But remember that the more excitement and comment you arouse by your attention-getters, the more attention your group will pay. So enlist the help of friends and move these toys into your assembly room, even though it may look like a toy shop!

The purpose is to show that just as a boy or girl progresses in skill as he learns to operate moving objects that go faster and faster, so the Christian is to develop certain skills if he is to grow ("go faster") in spiritual maturity.

Stroller or Baby Buggy

No effort is required for a baby or toddler to ride in a stroller! The responsibility is all on the mother, father, or older brother and sister. The child may jump up and down, squeal with delight, or try to climb out, but he has nothing

49

to do with propelling the stroller. Someone else does all the work.

Little Red Wagon

One of the first transportation toys a child learns to play with is a little wagon. See him as he grasps the handle and pulls the wagon across the room or down the sidewalk. He doesn't go very fast, and on his first few attempts he will stumble and fall. Later he learns to guide it, and may steer it quite successfully while going down a steep hill.

Scooter

With one foot on the scooter and one foot touching the sidewalk, a little fellow can scoot along at a fairly fast clip. But he's not likely to get a ticket for speeding!

Tricycle

At about the same age he learns to navigate a wagon, a youngster learns to ride a tricycle. This requires the coordination of both hands and both feet. He imagines he is driving a big truck, or that he is a patrolman, speeding down the highway to stop someone from driving recklessly. Later he will graduate to a bicycle, and maybe a motorbike. But the faster each toy becomes, the more skill and maturity are required.

Sled

Boys and girls enjoy sliding down long, steep hills in the winter. Those who are skilled in sledding learn to whiz along at remarkable speeds. Maneuvering the sled around sharp curves requires even more skill. Next it may be skis or a fast toboggan. The greater the speed, the greater the skill required.

Roller or Ice Skates

How many of you remember the first time you tried to skate? How many times did you fall down? Balance and coordination and self-confidence help to make a good skater. Champion skaters make it look easy, as they seem to glide effortlessly across the rink. They flash by at tremendous speed, and execute difficult and intricate turns.

You wouldn't expect a baby to win a gold medal for figure skating, and you wouldn't expect a teen-ager to ride in a stroller! Speed and skill come with maturity and practice.

Application

How are all these toys here at the front related to the Christian life? There is a basic principle in both. The faster and farther we go in the Christian life, the greater the skill that is needed.

How is "skill" measured in the Christian life?

First, one accepts Christ as Saviour and Lord. This is basic. No progress can be made until one first becomes as a little child, and trusts Christ with childlike humility and belief.

Second, one learns to accept responsibility. No one grows spiritually as long as he blames someone else for his failures. But as we accept responsibility for our own actions and assume responsible positions at home and in our church, we immediately start to grow. We "graduate" to a more sophisticated "toy."

Third, one must be on guard for the sins of the spirit. A professing Christian may be self-satisfied as long as he does not steal, lie, drink, gamble, or break the law. But growing Christians, those who progress at greater speeds, also guard against such faults as fear, jealousy, hate, prejudice, and envy.

Fourth, one must major on solving problems rather than aggravating them. He must be a part of the solution, not a part of the problem. You can spot a mature Christian in a minute: he is the kind who tackles problems head on with the idea of solving them rather than engaging in gossip, self-pity, or negative faultfinding.

Ephesians 4:14–15 advises us to "henceforth be no more children, tossed to and fro, and carried about with every wind of doctrine, . . . but speaking the truth in love . . . grow up into him in all things, which is the head, even Christ."

Hymns: "Give of Your Best to the Master"
            "Our Best"

Prayer: Some of us, O God, are still babes in Christ, expecting others to push us around in strollers. Help us to grow up in all things. Help us to do more for thee and for others, and to do it with greater speed. Save us from sloppiness, laziness, and procrastination. Amen.

12 How God Speaks to Us

Does God communicate with us? Multitudes of people will tell you that he does. Since God is a Spirit, how does he communicate with people living in a material world? I have three ordinary objects, and a person here to help illustrate how God speaks to us.

Letter or Telegram

When we want to send a message to a person who is far away, or when we want to make sure he understands every word, we send a written message. Often this is a letter or postcard. Sometimes it may be a telegram. Millions of printed and written messages go through the mails every day. Almost everyone enjoys going to the mailbox and finding a letter from a friend or relative.

God also uses the printed page to speak to us. The sixty-six books of our Bible contain his written message. Written in three languages (Hebrew, Aramaic, and Greek) over fifteen centuries by more than fifty authors of differing races and cultures, the Bible embraces five great civilizations. In its pages we find history, poetry, prophecy, philosophy, theology, oratory, humor, sarcasm, irony, music, drama, tragedy, strategy, biography, love stories, travelogues, laws, songs, prayers, letters, and genealogies.

Every day, millions turn to its pages for wisdom, comfort, reassurance, guidance, and knowledge. It is God's written method of communicating with us.

Telephone

(Check with your telephone company to see if you can borrow a telephone set. If not, use a toy set.)

There are more than 200,000,000 telephones in the world similar to the one I am holding before you. You can step to your own telephone and talk to someone in almost every nation in the world. The telephone is popular because it is personal, quick, and convenient. In addition to the enjoyment of receiving or sending a message, there is the added pleasure of hearing the voice of someone we love or know.

Does God dial us on the telephone? No, but many people do feel that he communicates with them in a personal way. Some call this intuition or insight. Others call it conscience. Others call it "leadership of the spirit," or "an impression," or "a feeling."

Some Christians are more deeply mystical than others. Whether or not you feel God has spoken to you personally, you can at least maintain an open mind to the possibility.

Potted Plant, Bouquet, or Box of Candy

A favorite way of communicating our love or friendship is to send a gift. It may be flowers on an anniversary or a box of chocolates on Valentine's Day. Whatever the gift, it is the sender's way of communicating a feeling or an emotion.

This must be one of God's favorite ways of communication, for he showers us with so many gifts. "Count your many blessings, see what God hath done." God speaks to us through the gift of our very own lives. He speaks through flowers and trees and birds that sing. He speaks through the beauty of nature and the stillness of the night. He speaks to us through the gift of friendship, the smile of a baby, the touch of a loved one. He speaks to us with warm clothing and a snug home in the winter. He speaks to us in all seasons with food and drink.

Sometimes these gifts are disguised in sorrow or disappointment. At first, we refuse them as blessings and call them tragedies, later to find that the illness or defeat we suffered was God's way of speaking to us. Some of us are so busy we could never hear God speak, except from a sick bed.

What is God trying to say to you and me through his gifts? Each must listen for himself, and interpret his gifts in the light of what he thinks is God's will for his life.

Ambassador

(This should be a man dressed in a business suit.)

The fourth object is not an object. It is a real, living person—a man. This man is an ambassador from our country. He represents our nation at the capitals of other nations. He is a personal envoy. Governments are not satisfied merely to exchange information by letter or telephone. Frequently, because of urgency or secrecy, a personal emissary is needed. That is why we have ambassadors.

God is not able to tell us everything through the Bible, through his gifts, or through insight and intuition. There comes a time when persons are needed to carry his message. But here the parallel ends. God did not send a person to represent himself to us. He came himself, in the form of a man. Jesus of Nazareth was God in the flesh. He was God here on earth, living and dying and suffering.

An ambassador is the closest object lesson we can think of. But an ambassador does not do full justice to what God communicates to us through Christ.

This is the meaning of Hebrews 1:1–2, "God, who at sundry times and in divers manners spake in time past unto the fathers by the prophets, hath in these last days spoken unto us by his Son."

Is God "getting through" to you in his efforts to communicate? Are you listening? Once it gets through to you, are you responding to the message?

Hymns: "Speak to My Heart"
            "Holy Bible, Book Divine"
            "Count Your Blessings"

Prayer: Open our eyes and ears, dear God, so that we can see and read the message you have for us. May we hear, whether you speak with the faintness of the chirping of a bird or the roar of thunder. Most of all, may we hear and receive Christ into our hearts, knowing that he is God himself at work in his world. Amen.

13 A Happy Balance

Preparation: In this program you will display several items of food which are rich in certain vitamins. The object is to show the value of a balanced diet for good health. The application is that Christians, rather than being one-sided, need balance and proportion in their lives.

Raw Carrot (Vitamin A)

Today we're going to talk about vitamins and nutrition. All of us know the value of a good diet. Good health depends on what we eat, as well as on exercise, rest, sunshine, fresh air, and a wholesome mental outlook.

Our nutrition may be good or poor, depending on the food we eat. Well-nourished persons have strong bones, muscles, and teeth, and healthy skin and blood. They feel good, have enough energy for their activities, and appear radiant and vigorous. Poor nutrition, commonly called malnutrition, results when a person eats too little food or the wrong kinds. Persons suffering from malnutrition may have decayed teeth, inflamed eyes, and dry hair. They are likely to be anemic, tired, listless, and may even suffer nervous disorders.

There are five major nutrients in a balanced diet: proteins, carbohydrates, fats, vitamins, and minerals. Our discussion will be limited to vitamins.

This carrot which I am holding is a rich source of vitamin A. So are broccoli, bananas, green beans, beef liver, and tomatoes. Vitamin A builds resistance to infection, keeps the skin healthy, and aids the eyes to function normally. It is essential for the growth of children and the development of babies before birth. Bone growth and normal tooth structure depend on it.

Oatmeal (Thiamine, a B vitamin)

If you like oatmeal or other whole-grain or enriched cereals, then you are likely to get the thiamine you need, which is one of the B vitamins. Thiamine is also found in pork, nuts, peas, and green vegetables. Like vitamin A, this vitamin is needed for growth. Thiamine gives you a good appetite and prevents fatigue.

Milk (Riboflavin, a B vitamin)

Riboflavin is another one of the B vitamins. It is most abundant in yeast, milk, liver, eggs, poultry, fish, and green and leafy vegetables. Riboflavin helps our bodies to use oxygen. When a person does not get enough riboflavin, cracks may develop in the skin at the corners of his mouth. He may get inflamed lips and a sore tongue, and scaliness of the skin around his nose and ears. His eyes may become very sensitive to light.

Orange (Vitamin C)

Since our bodies do not store vitamin C, it must be supplied daily in our diet. A good source is citrus fruits, such as this orange. It is also found in tomatoes, raw cabbage, strawberries, and cantaloupe. The Puerto Rican cherry has the highest concentration of vitamin C known. Without vitamin C, a person may have sore gums, hemorrhages under the skin, and general fatigue. Vitamin C strengthens the blood vessels and builds sound bones and teeth.

Egg (Vitamin D)

Vitamin D is not found in many of our common foods. It is present in butter, eggs, beef liver, and cow's milk.

This is a vitamin one must be careful about. Doctors have found that lack of vitamin D leads to serious bone changes. However, they have also found that excessive amounts of vitamin D also causes serious bone changes. (This is one good reason why no vitamins should be taken except on your doctor's advice.)

Application

I hope I haven't made you hungry with all this talk about food. The point I want to make is the value of a balanced diet. Remember that it is possible for a family to have an abundance of food, but still be undernourished because of poor choices of food. We sometimes see this in teen-agers who major on three or four favorite foods. They may gain or maintain weight on these foods, but they fail to get the basic nutrients for all-around good health.

Does this principle hold true in one's Christian life? By all means. Occasionally we see a well-meaning Christian whose life is stunted or one-sided.

It was said of Jesus that when he was here on earth he "increased in wisdom and stature, and in favour with God and man" (Luke 2:52). His was a well-balanced life. Although he lived a dedicated life, he did not spend all his time in prayer or in the Temple.

First, he increased in wisdom, or knowledge. Christians should be well-informed. They should read widely. They should try to make good grades in school. God does not place a premium on ignorance. He made you and me with an inquisitive mind, and one way to honor God is to use our minds to learn as much as possible about this intriguing universe in which we live.

Second, he increased in stature, or physical development. A Christian should try to be as robust and healthy as possible. Some people bring illness on themselves by poor habits of sleep, diet, and exercise. Others invite illness by their depressed, self-pitying attitude toward life.

Third, Jesus increased in favor with God, which means spiritual growth. Although conversion is an event that occurs when an individual puts his total trust in Christ as his Saviour, Christian growth is a lifetime adventure.

Fourth, Jesus increased in favor with man, or social poise and development. That is, people liked him. They enjoyed being with him and talking with him. He had many friends. A radiant Christian has friends. He attracts others with his personality. A sour disposition is no mark of consecration.

The key word in our discussion today is "balance." Is your

life balanced or one-sided? This is a question each of us must face, and each of us must find his own answer.

Hymns: "All the Way My Saviour Leads Me"
           "More Like the Master"
           "More Like Jesus Would I Be"

Prayer: We thank thee for Christ thy Son, the perfect man, who by his life demonstrated the fulness of the Godhead. Save us from spiritual malnutrition. Give us a balanced diet of thy grace and knowledge. Develop in us an interest in all of life about us. May the fulness and joyousness of our lives serve as a magnet to draw others to thee. Amen.

14 What Time Is It?

Preparation: Make a display of the six suggested clocks. If you know a friend whose hobby is collecting old clocks and watches, invite him to set up a display, too. You might not use his clocks in your presentation, but they would be an added appeal and focus attention on your devotional. The members of your group might enjoy browsing around the display, either before or after your meeting.

Wristwatch or Pocket Watch

Today we are talking about clocks. One of the most common is the wristwatch. Its basic purpose is to tell time. Some wristwatches even give the day of the month, too!

Persons who work by appointments or who travel a great deal need a watch more than those whose hours are fairly well regulated.

Cuckoo Clock or Antique Clock

Some clocks, such as this one, serve as conversation pieces more than as timepieces. They are often used as ornamental objects in homes. Visitors, attracted to them by the way they strike or by the intricate workmanship, comment and ask questions. Hence, we call them conversation pieces.

Perhaps you know someone whose hobby is collecting unique or antique clocks.

Time Clock

This is an important clock in businesses or plants where employees work and are paid by the hour. When an employee arrives for work, he checks in by "punching" the clock. He does the same when he leaves for lunch, and at the end of the day. On some jobs, employees check in and out for their coffee breaks.

At the end of the day, week, or pay period, the time clock shows exactly how many hours and minutes the employee spent on the job.

Time clocks are also used for security purposes. In large buildings such as hotels, a number of time clocks are dispersed on various floors. Every hour, a night watchman makes his rounds, punching the clock at each checkpoint. This shows whether he made his security checks regularly throughout the night.

Stopwatch

Here is a watch that is essential for most sporting events and athletic meets. With a time clock, a runner's or swimmer's speed can be timed to a fraction of a second. A time clock tells exactly when a basketball or football game is to end. A stopwatch is essential in any sport where the length of the game is controlled, or where individual performance is judged by the time it takes one to complete it.

Hourglass

In some kitchens you will find a miniature hourglass. Notice how this one is made which I am holding in my hand. At either end is a glass or plastic compartment, connected with a small aperture. When the hourglass is upended, the sand flows from the top compartment to the bottom. In a true hourglass, there is enough sand inside that a full hour is required for the sand to flow into the opposite end. Most of the ones we see in homes today are designed to measure one or three minutes.

Parents sometimes set a three-minute minder near the telephone, to remind their teen-agers to keep their calls to three minutes! A housewife may use one to time a three-minute egg. For most of us, they are more a novelty than anything else.

Alarm Clock

Everyone knows what this is for! If this is the exciting day we leave on a long-planned vacation, we are glad to hear the alarm. If it's a cloudy, rainy morning and we were up late the night before, we wish the alarm clock had never been invented.

Application

These clocks remind us of three significant Bible passages concerning time. The first is Psalm 90:12: "So teach us to number our days, that we may apply our hearts unto wisdom." Time is to be used wisely. It is not to be wasted. We are to make the most of our lives. We should number, or count, our days, and make the best of each one.

We also think of Psalm 56:3: "What time I am afraid, I will trust in thee." The story is told of a devout man who removed the twelve numerals from the face of his watch. In their place, he glued the twelve letters of the words, "Christ is Lord." Someone asked why. He answered, "I want to be reminded that whatever time of day or night it may be, Christ is still Lord." This kind of faith will remove fear any time we put it to practice.

Finally, let's read Psalm 90:4: "For a thousand years in thy sight are but as yesterday." We get tense and fretful if things do not work just the way we want them at exactly the time we desire, or if we make plans for certain events and certain days and are disappointed. It is reassuring to know that God is not limited to twenty-four hours a day, seven days a week, or 365 days a year. A thousand years in his sight are as one day. Time is on his side. He is not limited as we are. When life moves slowly, remember that God has eternity as well as time to achieve his goals. And as a Christian, you and I are on God's side, which means that eternity is ours, too!

Hymns: "Work, for the Night Is Coming"
             "When Morning Gilds the Skies"
             "Now the Day Is Over"

Prayer: Truly, O God, our times are in thy hands. Thou
             hast made us, and we are thine. Since our days are

numbered in this life, may we truly use them for thy glory. We thank thee for the days and for the nights, the weeks and the months, the years and the generations. In all of life and time, we recognize that Christ thy Son is truly Lord. In his name. Amen.

15 Looking Your Best

Preparation: This program should attract the attention of teen-agers and others who are style-conscious and anxious to make a good impression. Bring as many items as possible that are used for personal grooming. Bring those used both by men and women.

Make your impact by the sheer number of items. The more you can pile on a table in the front, the better.

The purpose of all the materials you see on this table is to make us look better! And that is certainly something most of us can stand.

Let's look at some of them. Here is a razor to make a man smooth-shaven, and a portable hair dryer a lady can use in her own home. And here is a nail clip, file, and some polish to clean, trim, and paint one's nails. Everyone needs a toothbrush and paste to keep his teeth sparkling. And speaking of brushes—look at some others. Here is a clothes brush to keep the lint off your suit, a shoe brush to shine your shoes, a hairbrush to manage your hair, and a complexion brush to clean your skin. And look at all the toiletries which make us look as well as smell better—colognes, hairdressing, makeup, perfume, soaps, powders, and so on.

(If you can think of other personal-care items from your own home or from a friend, bring them, too. The longer the list, the more impressive your point.)

Modern makeup and personal grooming can almost perform miracles these days. But there is a point beyond which they cannot go. It is illustrated in the old proverb, "Beauty is only skin deep." There is a beauty of personality and character that goes beyond one's physical appearance. All the grooming in the world cannot substitute for the lack of such.

Now it is true that personal grooming brings a certain amount of self-confidence. It gives one poise, so that his inner person has a better opportunity of showing itself. In *Hamlet* Shakespeare advised:

> Costly thy habit as thy purse can buy,
> But not express'd in fancy; rich, not gaudy;
> For the apparel oft proclaims the man.

But Shakespeare and all advertising to the contrary, clothing and makeup do not guarantee a pleasing personality. If they did, all the mannequins in the shop windows would suddenly burst into life!

A beautiful story in the Old Testament illustrates this. After the death of King Saul, God instructed the prophet Samuel to anoint a new king for Israel. God warned him not to base his judgment on physical appearance alone, "for the

Lord seeth not as man seeth; for man looketh on the outward appearance, but the Lord looketh on the heart" (1 Sam. 16:7).

Samuel went to the home of Jesse, the Bethlehemite. Jesse had eight sons, and Samuel thought that the first one he saw was worthy of being king. But God reminded him to look beyond personal appearance. Finally, he had looked at seven of the sons and refused each. Samuel asked Jesse if this were all. Rather apologetically, Jesse said he did have an eighth son, David, but that he was keeping the sheep. We remember the story—how Samuel anointed David, who later became one of the best-known of Israel's kings.

If Samuel had acted on his first impulse, his first impression, he would have chosen the first son. Acting wisely, he looked at the person as well as the personality, and chose David.

What does this tell us? First, that we should not prejudge a person until we really get to know him beneath the surface. Second, in building our own lives, we should not depend too heavily on mere physical appearance. Attractive people are those who act pretty as well as look pretty. The ultimate is what those beautifully manicured fingers *do,* what those tinted lips *say,* what that brain beneath the elaborate coiffure *thinks.* People who look right must first act right.

Hymns: "Let the Beauty of Jesus" (*Songs for Juniors*)
            "I Would Be True"
            "Truehearted, Wholehearted"

Prayer: We have learned, our Father, that some of the
            most attractive persons can be the cruelest at

heart, and some of the most repulsive-looking persons can have the warmest hearts and personalities. We thank thee for our bodies, and believe they are a trust from thee to keep well and strong, and to keep clean and attractive. But give us more than skin-deep beauty. Fill us with thy radiance, and may the warmth of our friendship shine through in every relationship. Amen.

16 Lord As Well As Saviour

As Christians, we frequently refer to Christ as our "Lord and Saviour." But do we really acknowledge Christ as our Lord with the same fervor that we accept him as our Saviour? Can he be our Saviour, unless he is also our Lord and Master? That is, expecting Christ to save us is impossible unless we are also willing for him to be the Master of our lives.

I hold in my hands some little metal objects which are far more important than their size would indicate. These objects are symbols of ownership and confidence. Yes, they are a bunch of keys. I use these keys to gain admission to important places. And I share these keys with family and friends whom I trust.

There is a sense in which a Christian gives to Christ the keys to every area of his life. Oh, not literal keys such as these; but we give him the authority, the leadership, to play the key role in every facet of our lives.

71

Car Key

Teen-agers get a big thrill on the day they receive a driver's license and have a set of car keys for their very own. And it is always a thrill to a person of any age when he holds in his hands the keys to a new car. Automobile keys are a symbol of mobility, of independence, of maturity. They make it easier for us to go where we wish, when we please.

If Christ is our Master, we are willing to trust our car keys to him. Again, don't take me literally! The Lord is not about to drive off with your car! What I mean is that we should seek his lordship, his will, in where we go and in how we drive our cars. We cannot truly claim to care about people if we endanger their lives by our driving habits. Nor can we truly claim Christ as our Master if we assume the prerogative to go wherever we please, whenever we please. Not that we have to be so trivial as to ask his will each time we drive around the block. But in the dedicated Christian's mind, there are no reserved times nor places. He gives to Christ the keys, the mastery, of how and where he drives.

House Keys

Have we given to Christ the keys of our homes? Discipleship is not merely going to church on Sunday. It includes putting Christian teachings into everyday practice.

Often, home is the hardest place to live our faith. We like to think of home as a place where we can let off steam and just be ourselves. And this is an important element in family life. But why not be "our Christian selves" instead of "just ourselves" ?

Unwittingly, we sometimes hurt most those we love the best. On the other hand, we love the most those whom we know the best. Parents, husbands and wives, and children are not saints, and should not pretend to be. We are all human beings, living in a human world, with other humans of similar limitations. But we can invite Christ to be the head of our families when we marry and on through life.

Safety-Deposit Key

Do you rent a safety-deposit box at the bank? Or, do you have a safe at home in which you keep valuables? Maybe you just have the locked drawer of a desk.

In any event, this key represents the material things in our lives on which we place great value. We protect them against theft or fire by locking them up. These valuables might include coin collections, financial papers such as bonds and stocks, deeds to property, heirlooms, jewelry, insurance policies, and the like.

Have we made Christ the Master of the *things* in our lives? I'm not talking about dropping an occasional dollar in the church offering plate, or even about tithing. I'm talking about the nine-tenths as well as the one-tenth. Is Christ truly the Master of all we own? Do we seek his will in how we earn our money, handle it, spend and give it, and, finally, in the manner we dispose of it at our deaths?

Office Key

This key symbolizes the place where we work, whether it be in an office, a schoolroom, a laboratory, or a plant.

Is Christ the Master of our vocations? Do we try just as hard to please him in our weekday work as we do in our Sunday worship?

Young people can seek the lordship of Christ in deciding on a career. Adults can seek his leadership when confronted with a job change. Everyone can use his daily work as an avenue of witnessing and service.

Friends may be more impressed with the genuineness of our profession by the way we work than by the way we worship.

Locker Key

If you are a student, you likely have a locker key for use at school. There you keep your gym clothes, books, and other personal objects. Let's use this key to symbolize one's recreational life and assume it opens a locker in the gym.

Leisure time is not "free" time in the sense it is ours to use as we please. The Christian never claims to be "free" in any area of life. If Christ is our Master, we are his slaves. Not that he wishes to exploit us, but that he wills our good in every aspect, including leisure time and recreation.

Hymns: "Since Jesus Came into My Heart"
          "More Like Jesus Would I Be"
          "More Like the Master"

Prayer: Our Father, we thank thee for Christ thy Son, whom we trust as our Saviour. We have not always been quick to acknowledge him as our Lord, and for this we ask thy forgiveness. May we give to him every key of our lives. May every door of our hearts and wills be open to his touch. Save us from hiding behind locked doors of indifference and pride. Amen.

17 The Family of Man

Someone once made the claim that if a group of people were displayed inside a cage at a zoo, they would attract more attention than any of the animals or birds!

Whether that statement is true or not, it is certain that people are interested in people. This helps explain a popular television program, *Candid Camera*.

So, for objects to illustrate certain truths today, we are going to use real, live people which, of course, are not objects at all, but rather personalities.

We will call them to stand here at the front, one by one.

Baby

Everyone loves a baby. The weakness of a baby reminds us of God's strength. A baby's youthfulness reminds us of God's agelessness. The warmth of a baby reminds us of God's tenderness and love. Especially at Christmas are we reminded that when God chose to reveal himself in the flesh, he chose the role of a baby. Christ came as an infant in Bethlehem's manger, not as a mighty warrior at the head of a great army.

One of our best-loved carols includes the prayer, "Be born in us today." Regardless of the season of the year, we can make it our prayer that Christ be born in us, regardless of our age.

Boy or Girl

This school-age youngster reminds us that when Jesus was only twelve, he showed interest in his mission to the world. On a trip with his parents to Jersualem, he became lost from them as he talked with the Temple officials. When Mary and Joseph showed concern, he asked, "Wist ye not that I must be about my Father's business?" (Luke 2:49).

A boy (or girl) such as the one standing here also reminds us of the childlike faith that is necessary for anyone who becomes a Christian. "Except ye be converted, and become as little children, ye shall not enter into the kingdom of heaven" (Matt. 18:3). We are not saved through childishness, but we do come to know Christ through childlike trust and faith.

Regardless of our age, unless we come to Christ with the childlike confidence of this youngster standing before us, we shall never find him. Christ hides himself from the proud and the self-sufficient.

Teen-ager

A teen-ager is neither adult nor child. A teener is a tweener. And I hope it will be no embarrassment to this teen-ager standing here for me to say that I am confident there are days when he feels as if he were still a child, and others when he feels as if he were already an adult!

Many characteristics of teen-agers could be cited. But let's take just one—that of quick growth. The teen years are the growing years. In a single year, a boy may gain several inches and suddenly find that none of last season's clothing fits anymore. At no other age does a person grow as much and as fast, physically, as in the teen years. Ask any mother who tries to feed one!

In the Christian life, there are some areas of growth that take a lifetime. But there are a few areas in which one should grow very quickly, like a teen-ager. Let's mention two or three.

We should grow quickly in our knowledge that this is God's world, and that for those who love him and seek to do his will, "all things work together for good" in the long run (Rom. 8:28). Unless we quickly come to this knowledge as Christians, we will waste precious time and energy in needless worry and frustration.

Second, we should grow quickly in our realization that life at the longest is brief. Whatever good we wish to accomplish must be done quickly, while there is time. The person who never develops any life goals, never gives himself to the accomplishment of them, will discover too late that life has slipped through his hands.

Adult

Here we see a mature person, perhaps a father or a mother. Many words could be used to describe adults, but let's settle for just one, the word "responsibility."

Adults feel the responsibility and pressures of their jobs. They feel responsible for their children—not only for their physical care but also for their spiritual and intellectual development. They feel responsible for offices they fill in the community and church. Many of them feel responsible for aged parents or grandparents.

In the Christian life, unfortunately, some never reach the middle years of responsibility. We may accept Christ in childlike faith but still retain a great deal of childishness as far as emotional maturity is concerned. Not all the children in a typical church are in their early teens or younger. Some "children" are thirty, forty, and even fifty years of age.

That is why Ephesians 4:14–15 pleads that "we henceforth be no more children, tossed to and fro, and carried about with every wind of doctrine, . . . but speaking the truth in love, may grow up."

Every Christian should have a goal of becoming a mature, "adult" Christian—one who is willing to assume responsibility, carry his share of the load, and forget little petty grievances that might upset a child but have no place in the emotional and spiritual maturity of adulthood.

Senior Adult

Our attitudes toward senior adults are quickly changing. More and more, we are realizing that some of the best years of one's life come during retirement. Retirees are not only living longer, they are also living better, due to improved medical care.

Senior adults do not want a rocking chair in the corner. Rather, they want to feel a part in the real world about them.

Maybe not as active a part as they once knew, but a real one, nonetheless.

What do senior adults have to offer? We can think of several contributions, but let's talk about wisdom. The only way to get wisdom is through experience. One can earn all kinds of graduate degrees through the assimilation of knowledge and facts. But wisdom is more than facts and learning. Wisdom includes insights and judgments acquired in the school of hard knocks.

Unfortunately, a few senior adults have a sour, pessimistic outlook on everything. But there are many who can make rich contributions through sharing their wisdom gained from a lifetime of experiences.

Likewise, in the Christian life, it is not enough just to memorize the books of the Bible or be able to describe in detail the missionary journeys of Paul. A Christian needs wisdom and insight. For such wisdom, Christians of all ages should seek and pray. James 1:5 promises, "If any of you lack wisdom, let him ask of God, that giveth to all men liberally, and upbraideth not; and it shall be given him." Although certain measures of spiritual wisdom come only with age, this passage of Scripture assures us that all believers can seek it, and that God will not "upbraid" or ridicule any who seek such.

Where and how do we need wisdom? It would take an encyclopedia to answer that, because we need wisdom everywhere we turn—in rearing our children, in solving marital problems, in dealing with our neighbors, in working on the job, in serving our church, in getting along with other nations of the world.

There is no lack of knowledge—especially technological knowledge, which has experienced such a rapid spurt in recent years. But there is, and always will be, need for wisdom and judgment and insight. Remember that Jesus, as a boy, increased in wisdom as well as in knowledge and physical stature (cf. Luke 2:52).

Hymns: "Open My Eyes That I May See"
"In Christ There Is No East or West"
"Rise Up, O Men of God"

Prayer: O God, in the mirror of mankind, we see ourselves. We see ourselves in the smile of a baby, the laughter of a child, the daring of a teen-ager, the strength of an adult, the maturity of old age. From the best of these various ages may we select lasting traits that will strengthen our own lives and bless those to whom we minister. Amen.

18 People Count, Too

Presentation: For this presentation you bring actual, live pets to your meeting place! This will require ingenuity and planning, but the curiosity and interest you arouse will be worth the effort.

You might enlist members of your group to help, by asking those who have pets to bring them. Each can give a brief description of his pet, using the material that follows, or making up his own talk.

Dog

Dog has been "man's best friend" for centuries. These friendly, obedient animals serve people throughout the world in work, play, and sport.

Some owners breed dogs for sale and profit. Others keep them for companionship or protection. Sportsmen use them for hunting. Dogs range in size from the Chihuahua, which is not much larger than a pigeon, to the Irish wolfhound, which may stand three feet high at the shoulders. Mastiffs and St. Bernards, the heaviest dogs, weigh as much as 180 pounds.

Stone-age people who lived in Europe tamed dogs ten to twenty thousand years ago to track game. About eight thousand years ago, the ancient Egyptians raised greyhound-like dogs. And here in North America, the Indians tamed dogs as early as four thousand years ago.

Aquarium

Many people enjoy keeping fish in aquariums in their own homes. Compared with many pets, fish require little care. And they don't make any noise!

Goldfish are perhaps the most popular. Centuries ago, the Japanese and Chinese bred goldfish to produce beautiful colorings and unusual fins and body forms. Goldfish were brought to Europe in 1611. Today, there are one hundred fancy varieties, but only about twenty kinds are sold.

Goldfish are only one of many varieties of sea life which can be bred in a home aquarium. In a balanced aquarium, several varieties of both animals and plants are bred. Each helps the other. The goldfish, sunfish, darter, ramshorn snail, Japanese snail, and pond snail give off the gas, carbon dioxide. The plants—such as elodea, vallisneria, and cabomba—use this gas and in turn give off oxygen, which the animals breathe.

Of still more interest are the large public aquariums, such as the John G. Shedd Aquarium in Chicago, the nation's largest and best-equipped, with 138 permanent tanks and 65 balanced aquariums.

Cat

The cat is a popular house pet and one of the smartest animals. He makes a faithful, friendly companion, but he is independent and wants his way!

Phoenician traders, carrying Egyptian cats in their ships, probably brought the first domesticated cats to Europe about 900 B.C. European colonists brought domestic cats to the Americas in the 1700's.

The eyes and whiskers of cats are very interesting. Cats cannot see in complete darkness, as many persons believe. But they can see in extremely dim light, since the iris of their eyes opens wider than it does in the eyes of man or any other animal.

Their long whiskers are delicate sense organs. Most cats have from twenty-five to thirty of them, which grow in four rows from the side of the mouth to above the eyes. The whiskers are attached to nerves in their skin, and they help cats feel their way through bushes and avoid walls and trees. Cats even touch whiskers with each other to "talk" back and forth!

Caged Birds

About nine thousand species of birds, many of which are valuable to man, live throughout the world. Chickens, turkeys, and other poultry provide meat and eggs. Birds help the farmer by eating insects that would harm trees and crops. They scatter the seeds of wild fruits, other plants, and trees. Scientists believe, for example, that many of the white-oak forests were "planted" by blue jays.

Birds have been popular as pets since ancient times for their singing and beauty. Canaries are bred for their songs and bright colors. Parakeets and parrots are popular as talking birds (although crows, ravens, mynahs, and starlings also can be trained to talk).

Many parakeets and some canaries, become so tame that they fly about the house. Pet pigeons can be taught to do tricks and antics, and to carry messages.

Application

Doubtless you have wondered about the purpose of bringing these pets to this service. They do have a lesson for us, and a very important one. The basic truth or lesson here is that God loves and cares for the beautiful plant and animal life of this world. Genesis 1:31 says, "God saw every thing that he had made, and, behold, it was very good."

Some people criticize others for spending so much time and energy on pets and other animals. But the birds and fish and animals are a part of God's creation, and he considers them "very good."

Now look at this verse: "Behold the fowls of the air: for they sow not, neither do they reap, nor gather into barns; yet your heavenly Father feedeth them. Are ye not much better than they?" (Matt. 6:26).

Our reassurance is that if God is so concerned even with the birds of the air and the "grass of the field" (Matt. 6:30), how much more concerned is he for us? Not a sparrow falls without his knowledge. And you and I are worth far more in his sight than a sparrow!

(If the pets suggested are not available, select others,

such as hamsters, ducks, and white mice. If yours is a children's group, each boy and girl may be encouraged to bring his own pet. But do anticipate the possible confusion of mixing cats and dogs!)

Hymns: "This Is My Father's World"
          "God Will Take Care of You"
          "All Creatures of Our God and King"
          "For the Beauty of the Earth"

Prayer: We remember, our Father, that thy Son was born in a manger, surrounded by the animals of the stable. We recall how he made his triumphal entry into Jerusalem, riding on a colt. And we know that when the floods threatened the ancient world, thou didst instruct Noah to provide safety for all the birds and animals. Truly, this is thy world, and the work of thy hands. Most of all, we are grateful that you care for us, and that even the hairs of our head are numbered. As we see the sky blackened with the thousands of migrating birds in the fall months, may it remind us that each is known by thee, and that each of us is known far better. Amen.

19 The Living Word

Presentation: Arrange a Bible display. Ask members to bring any Bibles they might have which are unusual for their age, size, translation, version, or history. A nearby book store or library may loan you some copies. Also ask your pastor for any distinctive Bibles he may own.

Point out interesting features of as many of the Bibles as possible. You may or may not use the following suggestions. Feel free to be original, and focus on the Bibles in your particular display. Enlist others to help you. But do save time for the application.

Encourage members to browse at the tables, both before and after the service. Better still, make the display available to other groups in your church by moving it to a hallway or other prominent place.

Small, White Bible

Tiny, white Bibles are often presented as gifts to new babies. Brides often carry a white Bible, intertwined with white satin and tiny flowers. A white Bible suggests purity, and tells that the life of the baby, or the home of the new bride, is to be founded on the Word of God.

Large, Pulpit Bible

A pulpit Bible serves largely for ornamental purposes. Displayed prominently on the pulpit or communion table, it is a silent reminder that the Word of God is central in worship, that we gather to hear the Word preached and taught.

In some churches a ritual is used at the beginning of the service to open the pulpit Bible. At the end of the service there is a formal closing of the Book. Again, this is a symbol that the people have gathered to open and hear the Bible.

Family Bible

Here is an old family Bible. You will be interested in examining the handwriting on these pages which lists the births, deaths, and marriages of this particular family.

Family Bibles are not as popular as they once were, since better public records are now kept of births, deaths, and marriages. But before birth records were kept, entries in the family Bible were considered authoritative. Older persons still use the family Bible to verify their birth date for Social Security records.

Soul-Winner's New Testament

Some Christians never leave home without a New Testament in their pocket, purse, or glove compartment. Some businessmen keep a New Testament prominently displayed on their desks. These are often used for personal witnessing, or for reading a verse of encouragement and hope to a friend who is facing a crisis.

A pocket New Testament tells us that the Word is not bound to the pulpit but that it is the Word for the people, to be used in everyday life as well as formal worship.

Metal-plated New Testament

These are very popular as gift items in wartime. A few soldiers have returned with the metal covers of such Bibles dented from a bullet. They credit their lives to such a Bible, saying that it deflected a bullet that otherwise would have entered their bodies.

However, we must avoid any tendency to look upon the Bible as a good luck charm. The message inside the covers is far more important than the covers themselves.

Good News for Modern Man*

There seems to be no end to the number of very fine translations and versions of the Scriptures. As words and their meanings change, the Bible needs to be changed accordingly. By this we do not mean a change in the basic meaning of the Scriptures, but simply using the words and phrases that are current to express the age-old message of truth.

One of the most popular of the recent translations is this *Good News for Modern Man,* which I am holding. The popularity of this translation has far exceeded the most

---

* *The New Testament in Today's English Version,* © American Bible Society, New York, New York, 1966.

ambitious dreams of the publisher, the American Bible Society, and the translator, Robert G. Bratcher.

Good News was intended for the 10 million Americans who don't read well or who are learning English as a second language. It contains a three-thousand-word common language vocabulary, words that are spoken by nearly everyone. But Bratcher succeeded so well in recapturing the New Testament in the plain, everyday language of the man on the street that it became an immediate best seller.

First published in September, 1966, it went through twenty-one printings in twelve months, for a total of 6.5 million copies. This popular paperback New Testament is illustrated with about two hundred modern line drawings by Swiss artist Annie Vallotton. Bratcher credits at least half of the translation's success to these "eye-catching and revealing" illustrations.

Application

Old Bibles, new Bibles, rare Bibles, tiny Bibles, white Bibles, and red Bibles! Take your pick—they are available in hundreds of formats.

But the best Bibles are not printed and bound. Rather, they are engraved permanently and indelibly in our minds and characters. That is the meaning of Psalm 119:11, "Thy word have I hid in mine heart, that I might not sin against thee."

It is helpful to display a pulpit Bible or a family Bible in a prominent place for all to see. It is impressive to keep an open Bible on one's desk, or for a bride to carry one as she approaches the marriage altar. But none of these can substitute for the Word of God as it comes alive through our personalities.

"After those days, saith the Lord, I will put my law in their inward parts, and write it in their hearts; and will be their God, and they shall be my people. . . . they shall teach no more every man his neighbour, and every man his brother, saying, Know the Lord: for they shall all know me, from the least of them unto the greatest" (Jer. 31:33–34).

Hymns: "Holy Bible, Book Divine"
         "Word of God, Across the Ages"
         "Thy Word Is a Lamp to My Feet"
         "Thy Word Is Like a Garden, Lord"

Prayer: Give us the wisdom to understand thy Word, O Lord, but most of all, give us the grace to practice it. Amen.

20 What About Tomorrow?

Preparation: Weather forecasting goes back at least to Jesus' time. In Matthew 16:2–3 we read, "When it is evening, ye say, It will be fair weather: for the sky is red. And in the morning, It will be foul weather to-day: for the sky is red and lowering."

In this program, you will display four or five of the basic tools used by meteorologists in predicting the weather. These objects will not be as easy to locate as most suggested in this book. If you have a friend who is interested in meteorology, or there is a weather forecasting station near you, these may help. For general background, look up "weather" or "weather forecasting" in a good encyclopedia.

There are four main elements in weather: temperature, wind, moisture, and air pressure. You will display the instruments used to measure these four.

Temperature

Temperature affects the weather more than anything else, and it is the easiest to measure. Here you see a common thermometer, which most of us have around our homes. To find the correct temperature, we place the thermometer in a shady spot.

The sun sends huge amounts of energy into space, some of which, in the form of sunshine, reaches the earth. Some of this energy is absorbed and changed into heat, and the varying intensity of this heat vitally affects our changing weather.

Wind

Wind, which is simply the movement of air over the surface of the earth, is an important factor in weather conditions. A soft breeze may make a pleasant summer day. A violent windstorm may bring injuries, death, and property destruction.

Here are two instruments to measure the wind. The first is the most familiar—a weather vane, to show the direction from which the wind is blowing.

The second is the anemometer. Note it has long spokes with cups attached to them. The wind makes the cups whirl around. Meteorologists calculate wind speed by how fast or slow the cups move. In the United States, wind speed is stated in miles per hour.

Moisture

Moisture may fall to earth as rain, snow, hail, or sleet. Or, it may remain in the atmosphere as humidity. To measure the humidity, you can use a psychrometer, such as the one I am holding. Note it consists of two thermometers set on a support that can be whirled in the air. The bulb of one thermometer is covered with a wet cloth. Humidity is measured by the contrasting temperatures in the two thermometers after the moisture in the wet cloth evaporates.

To measure the amount of rainfall or snowfall, we use this cylindrical instrument called a rain gauge. The inches of rain or snow can be measured by the amount that drops into a long, narrow tube inside the gauge. Snow that falls into the tube may be melted and measured as rain, or it may be weighed. (A 6-inch layer of moist snow or a 30-inch layer of dry snow equals about one inch of rain.)

Air Pressure

Variations in temperature affect the weight of the air, and the weight of the air pushing down on the earth varies from time to time and from place to place. Warm air weighs less than cold air, and exerts less pressure on the earth, hence an area of low pressure. Cold air, which is heavier, presses harder and creates an area of high pressure. The "highs" and "lows" vitally affect weather changes.

Note this barometer, which measures air pressure. This is simply a long glass tube with its open end in a cup of mercury. As the air pressure changes, so does the height to which the mercury rises in the tube.

Making the Forecast

Forecasting the weather with any degree of accuracy is a highly sophisticated art, and requires the careful analysis of all four factors: temperature, pressure, humidity, and winds.

If this brief discussion has stimulated your interest, you might like to cultivate meteorology as a hobby, or even as a career. About three hundred weather stations in the United States and its possessions employ full-time staffs. Besides, the U.S. Weather Bureau has over twelve thousand cooperating substations that furnish information to the principal offices.

Application

How is weather forecasting related to the Christian life? The relationship is one of principle, not technique. And the principle is this: Your life and mine can be predicted on the basis of how we are living today (the same as tomorrow's weather can be predicted on the basis of today's conditions).

Far out over the Pacific and along the upper reaches of Canada, certain weather conditions are developing today (wind, moisture, pressure, temperature) which will dominate our weather next week. Once the forces are set in motion, no known methods can stop the inexorable march of weather.

The principle is stated in Galatians 6:7, "Whatsoever a man soweth, that shall he also reap." What we shall be tomorrow, we are becoming today. Life's directions and purposes change slowly. Once the bent of one's life and interests is set, it is not easily changed. Look carefully at yourself in a mirror. What you see today is basically the person you will see tomorrow.

We like to fool ourselves, saying we can indulge in this or that, but that we are going to straighten up and be a better person tomorrow. Highly unlikely! The seed we are sowing today is the fruit that will be picked tomorrow.

Fortunately, this works both ways. If we are headed in the right direction today, we are more assured of the proper destination tomorrow. If we are headed wrong today, we will be wrong tomorrow. Sobering, but true.

Hymns: "Building, Daily Building" (*Songs for Juniors*)
          "Fight the Good Fight"
          "My Soul, Be on Thy Guard"
          "Truehearted, Wholehearted"

Prayer: Dear Father, help us plant the kind of seeds today that will produce flowers instead of thorns tomorrow. Amen.

21 Christ in Art

Preparation: Warner Sallman has been one of the most popular religious artists since World War II. He is best known for his Head of Christ, *which has been widely reproduced throughout the world. Many churches have prints of his paintings in their buildings. Others are found in homes, on calendars, and on greeting cards. It will not be difficult to locate four or five of his paintings to use for this devotional.*

The larger your group, the larger the print will need to be for maximum viewing. Simply hold up the pictures before your group. Or, use an opaque projector for small prints which you wish to project on a screen. Colored slides of these paintings may be even more effective. If you are working with children, pass the pictures around so they can hold them in their own hands and study them closely. Or allow them to stand beside you and examine the pictures for themselves.

(If you have difficulty locating prints of Sallman's paintings, consult your Baptist Book Store. If this is not possible,

*write direct to the exclusive distributor of his works, Kriebel
and Bates, Inc., 4125 N. Keystone, Indianapolis, Indiana
46205, and ask for a catalog of Sallman art.*)

Introduce your devotional with the following comment:
"How did Christ look when he was here on earth? No one
knows. Photography was unknown in the first century. And
we have no contemporary art in existence by an artist of his
day. But hundreds of artists have tried to express their concepts. We have for you five prints of paintings by Warner
Sallman. Each is well-known, and doubtless you have one
or more of them in your home. Each has a distinct message
for us."

If you wish, enlist five persons to help, each of whom will
discuss one picture.

Christ Our Pilot

This is an interesting picture because it presents both a
contemporary person and Christ. At the wheel of the ship
at sea is a strong young man with broad shoulders and dark
hair, wearing a red shirt. He is peering intently ahead. The
waves in the background suggest a storm at sea.

Overshadowing the sailor is the figure of Christ. One hand
rests gently on the boy's shoulder. The other points ahead,
as if to show the young man where to steer the vessel to
safety through the storm.

We frequently talk about the "sea of life," which suggests
that life *is* much like an ocean voyage. There are days when
the seas are calm and the sun shines brightly. Too, there are
dark nights of stormy seas and wind and lightning. Whatever

our course or destination, each of us feels more secure with
a hand on our shoulders. That is why we appreciate the
following hymn, which I want us to sing together as we
focus our eyes on the painting (slide):

> Jesus, Saviour, pilot me
> Over life's tempestuous sea;
> Unknown waves before me roll,
> Hiding rock and treach'rous shoal;
> Chart and compass came from Thee:
> Jesus, Saviour, pilot me.

> As a mother stills her child,
> Thou canst hush the ocean wild;
> Boist'rous waves obey Thy will
> When Thou say'st to them, "Be still";
> Wondrous Sov'reign of the sea,
> Jesus, Saviour, pilot me.

The Good Shepherd

Here is another well-known Sallman painting, that of
Christ with a staff in one hand and holding a small lamb in
the other. Gathered around him are the sheep of his flock.
Peaceful mountains form a colorful backdrop.

Note how the eyes of Christ are fastened on the one little
lamb in his arms. Does this suggest the parable of the lost
sheep? Is this the one that was lost, for whose sake Christ
left the other ninety-nine safe in the fold while he sought
it out?

It could be. But most of us identify this painting with
Psalm 23. It also suggests John 10:14–16, "I am the good
shepherd, and know my sheep, and am known of mine. . . ."

And other sheep I have, . . . them also I must bring."

Most of us know Psalm 23 by memory. As we look at the picture, let us quote it together.

The Lord is my shepherd; I shall not want. He maketh me to lie down in green pastures: he leadeth me beside the still waters. He restoreth my soul: he leadeth me in the paths of righteousness for his name's sake. Yea, though I walk through the valley of the shadow of death, I will fear no evil: for thou art with me; thy rod and thy staff they comfort me. Thou preparest a table before me in the presence of mine enemies: thou anointest my head with oil; my cup runneth over. Surely goodness and mercy shall follow me all the days of my life: and I will dwell in the house of the Lord for ever.

(Or, ask a soloist to sing this psalm, which has been adapted for music by James Montgomery. It is on page 57 of the *Baptist Hymnal*.)

Christ at Heart's Door

Here is another favorite—Christ knocking at a door, on which there is no handle. Weeds seem to cover the entrance, as if it has been a long time since the door was used by anyone.

The meaning is evident: Christ knocks patiently at the door of one's life. But he does not force his way inside. The door opens from the inside. One must voluntarily receive Christ. "As many as received him, to them gave he power to become the sons of God" (John 1:12).

If we could force people into the kingdom of God, we might set forth with armed might to drive sinners into heaven. But no one is drafted into the army of the Lord.

Each is a volunteer. Each decides for himself to unlock the door from the inside, to admit the heavenly guest.

If anyone present has never accepted Christ as his personal Saviour, will you right now accept the promise of Revelation 3:20–21?

Behold, I stand at the door, and knock: if any man hear my voice, and open the door, I will come in to him, and will sup with him, and he with me. To him that overcometh will I grant to sit with me in my throne, even as I also overcame, and am set down with my Father in his throne.

Christ in Gethsemane

Here is another painting that has inspired millions—the Lord using a pile of rock as an altar in Gethsemane, with his face turned imploringly to heaven. Note how his hands are grasped together in front of him, suggesting both strength and resignation as he makes a final plea for deliverance from the cross—yet makes himself unreservedly available. The purple robe suggests another robe of purple which the soldiers will, that same night, throw over his shoulders as a mockery of his supposed kinship.

Christ in Gethsemane reminds us of the anguish he suffered for us. His prayer is also an example to us, a reminder that we too can find inner peace when, without reservation, we give ourselves over to God's will. "And he went a little farther, and fell on his face, and prayed, saying, O my Father, if it be possible, let this cup pass from me: nevertheless not as I will, but as thou wilt" (Matt. 26:39).

Are we able to pray that prayer?

The Head of Christ

Sallman's *Head of Christ* is saved for the last because it seems to embody the whole of Jesus' personality and ministry.

Note how the face combines youth and maturity; the vision and daring of youth are tempered with the wisdom and experience of age. This painting suggests such words as dedication, faith, confidence, courage, and purity.

What passage of Scripture does this picture suggest to you? (Allow time for answers, if in a small group.) What about Luke 2:52? "And Jesus increased in wisdom and stature, and in favour with God and man." Our Lord was intelligent ("wisdom"). He was strong and manly ("stature"). He was dedicated ("favour with God"). He was well liked by his friends ("favour with man").

If we are truly like Christ, we will strive for excellence in a well-rounded life of strong physical health, a well-trained and disciplined mind, consecration, and an ability to get along with and be liked by others.

Hymns: See suggestions above.

Prayer: Father God, we know that no artist is able to depict thy Son as he really was. What we have seen is one man's opinion. Yet his face surely mirrored compassion, his hands surely showed concern, his shoulders undoubtedly suggested strength, his eyes must have reflected concern for all whom he saw. Help us not to be so concerned with how Christ looked here on earth, but with what others think of Christ today as they see him in us. May we by our deeds and words show to others that Christ is living, that he loves everyone, and that his shoulders and arms are strong enough to carry every lost sheep to the safety of the heavenly fold. Amen.

22 Old Testament Heroes

Preparation: For this program, select four persons to help you, who will be dressed in costumes similar to those worn in Bible times. The manner in which each person dresses is the device to attract attention.

Children's groups will enjoy this, for they like to dress up and make believe. Adults, too, will be intrigued by the unique nature of this devotional.

In a sense, this devotional is a drama. There are four speaking parts. These need not be memorized. They will be more effective if spoken informally, in one's own words.

Use your imagination to put together attention-getting costumes. Ask your friends to search their closets—you will be amazed how odds and ends of clothing, scarves, headpieces, jewelry, and so on can be utilized.

Joseph: A Lad Who Dreamed

I am sure there is no need for me to call attention to this coat of many colors which I am wearing. My father gave it to me, because I was his favored son. It is a mark of distinction. When I put it on, I felt very proud. Perhaps I was guilty of showing off in front of my eleven brothers.

You will remember from the Bible that I had many dreams. Eventually, my dreams got me into trouble. Or maybe it was the fact I bragged too often about my dreams. On one occasion, I dreamed that eleven stars, the sun, and the moon obeyed me. Evidently my brothers feared that they would have to bow down to me, for they sold me as a slave into Egypt.

There, my interest in dreams saved me from slavery, because I interpreted one of the Pharaoh's dreams about a forthcoming drought. To make a long story short, I was used of God to save my father's family from starvation during the famine.

No doubt I played the show-off in boasting to my brothers. Life would have been more pleasant in our family had I taken my place alongside my brothers, rather than trying to be the star.

But I do not regret my dreams, for where there are no dreams and visions, the people truly perish. What are *your* dreams for tomorrow?

Methuselah

Can you tell by the lines in my face, my stooped shoulders, and these outdated clothes that I am Methuselah, the oldest-known person ever to live?

You will not find much in the Old Testament about me. In fact, my name is mentioned only two or three times. My only claim to distinction is that I lived a long, long time. Genesis 5:27 simply says that I died after living 969 years.

What I accomplished during those 969 years is hidden from you, for no records were kept. My reason for appearing before you today is to say that life is not measured just by length. Merely to live a long time does not guarantee that one has lived well. Life has height and depth and breadth as well as length. Some people live short lives, but in that time accomplish untold good. Others live many years, with nothing more to be said than, "He died at the age of so-and-so."

Ideally, one should live long and live well. But if faced with a choice, it is better to live well and die young, than to live long but meaninglessly. Jesus' earthly ministry was only thirty-three years, but who can measure the depth and breadth and height of his influence?

Miriam, the Sister of Moses

You will notice from the way I am dressed that I am a young maiden, living in slavery in Egypt. My clothing is not expensive, for our life in Egypt was harsh and bitter. Often we were forced to make brick without straw, and piece together what rags we could find for clothing, or wear hand-me-downs.

You will also notice this wicker basket I am holding, and the tiny baby [use a doll] inside. He is my little brother. My mother used tar to make the basket watertight. Actually, it is now a little boat.

Pharaoh, our ruler, has said that each male baby is to be thrown into the river as soon as he is born. We want to save our baby brother Moses.

If you have read the book of Exodus in the Old Testament,

you know how the story turns out. Pharaoh's daughter finds this little baby, loves him, and designates our mother as the nurse. Later, when Moses is a man, he delivers our people from Egyptian slavery. Through him, God gave my people the Law, including the Ten Commandments.

My job doesn't sound exciting—hiding here in the bulrushes near the river, watching a baby. But because I took my job seriously, staying here regardless of how hot the sun bore down, I was used of God to save the life of a baby of destiny.

How about you? Are you faithfully doing the work God has asked you to do?

Samuel

(Note: Use a boy of about twelve years of age. He will be wearing night clothes typical of Bible times, which probably consisted of a simple robe worn also by day. His hair should be tousled, and he should wear sandals. He may carry an oil lamp and begin by yawning to convey sleepiness.)

My parents, Elkanah and Hannah, were very old when I was born. They were so grateful when God blessed them with a son that they named me Samuel, which means "asked of God." When I was still a baby, they dedicated me to God in the Temple.

I have been living here in the temple with Eli, the priest. I am sleepy tonight because three times I have been wakened by someone calling my name. Each time I ran to Eli, but he said he didn't call. This last time, he told me to answer, "Speak, Lord; for thy servant heareth." When I lie down again, if I hear this voice, I am going to do what Eli said.

(The Narrator now speaks.)

And that is exactly what Samuel did. When a voice called his name a fourth time, he acknowledged it as being from God. In return, he received a vision of how he would be used of God.

Later in life, Samuel was chosen to anoint the first king of Israel, a youth by the name of Saul. Doing God's will later in life depended on willingness while he was young. Samuel is an everlasting reminder to us that God can speak to youngsters, that they can hear him speak, and that he can then begin to reveal his purposes for their lives. As a boy, Samuel did not see clearly all that was to be expected of him. But he entered each door as it opened—which is all that any of us can do, whether we are eight or eighty.

You can easily expand this devotional by selecting other characters from the Old Testament. Or, you can plan two or more devotionals, since there is almost no limit to the number of characterizations possible from the Old Testament. You can write, or improvise, your own copy, and design the simple costumes needed.

Hymns: "I Heard the Voice of Jesus Say"
            "Footsteps of Jesus"

Prayer: Out of the past, O God, thou hast spoken to us through these men and women of history. Help us to avoid their mistakes, imitate their virtues, and in every crisis of life, seek thy will first and always. Amen.

23 New Testament Heroes

(*These Went Free!*)

Preparation: This devotional is similar to the one preceding, only here you are dealing with characters from the New Testament. Also, the four suggested are grouped under a common theme, "These Went Free!"

As with the Old Testament heroes, you can add to the list, substitute, or even work up additional devotionals. The Bible is filled with interesting people! You could easily find enough to last several weeks.

If you have not already read chapter 22, go back and do so for helpful ideas that are applicable here.

Zacchaeus: Freed from Greed

Can you tell who I am by my size and the way I am dressed? Note that I am a short man, and that I am dressed in expensive clothing of New Testament times. Yes, you guessed correctly. I am Zacchaeus, the man who made so much money collecting taxes. The only drawback was that I was not always honest. I took advantage of people, charged higher taxes than they owed, and pocketed the difference.

But Jesus spoke in my community one day. There was such a crowd, I climbed into a tree to see. I'll have to admit it was largely out of curiosity. I had no intention of changing my ways, because I was a chief collector, and had amassed a fortune as head collector at the important road center of Jericho. But this Jesus was so friendly he even invited himself to my home for a meal.

This impressed me, because eating with an unpopular publican was contrary to the social customs of the day. Out of this friendship, I was converted to Christianity. My conscience bothered me so much that I promised right then to give half of my fortune to the poor, and to restore fourfold to anyone I had overcharged.

I am not bragging about this, for it is no more than I should have done. Yes, Christ freed me. He set me free from greed and gave me a new purpose in life. Now I care about people, not just how much money I can get out of them.

Lazarus: Freed from Death

Don't let me frighten you by the way I am dressed, or by the pale, ghostly look of my face. I was wrapped in these graveclothes for burial, following a serious illness and subsequent death. My sisters, Mary and Martha, sent word to our good friend, Jesus. But for some reason, he did not come. They were greatly disappointed, for they knew he could have gotten there before I died, if he wished.

Then today he did come. He gave instructions to roll back the big stone that blocked the entrance to the burial cave. Then in a loud voice, he cried for me to come forth from the dead. When I first gained consciousness and saw the

Lord, I noticed that he had been crying. Some said he cried over the lack of faith of my sisters. Others said he was crying over my death. Whatever the reason, it reassured me that he is a Saviour who cares, and who can be moved by the feelings of people.

What Christ did here today has demonstrated two things. First, he showed his humanity by shedding real tears. Second, he proved his divinity by raising the dead. If he were not human, he would not have cried. Were he not divine, he could never have brought life back to my dead body.

Now all of us truly know what he meant when he said, "I am the resurrection, and the life: he that believeth in me, though he were dead, yet shall he live" (John 11:25).

Legion: Freed from Demons

If you knew what I have been through, you would not condemn the way I look. Yes, there are chains around my ankles and wrists. Yes, I have almost torn my clothes into shreds. I was demon-possessed. I was insane. Many devils lived inside me, all at one time. They drove me mad.

My family and townspeople chained me out in the cemetery. But in my fury, I was often strong enough to break the chains. In the night of my despair, I would scream and pull my hair. Then Jesus came, and commanded those devils to enter a herd of swine. How free I felt when that spirit of insanity left me, and I was sober, and in my right mind.

I was so impressed that I asked permission to become one of Jesus' followers, and to work with him. But he told me I would be more useful in my hometown, among people who knew me before my healing. I guess he thought others might not believe my story. But my own people will—because they can't help but see the change in me. I am on my way home now, and once I am dressed presentably and rested from my ordeal, I will give myself to others who are bound in chains of one kind or another.

A Woman Freed from Passion

You do not know my name. It is just as well you don't. It is not given in the Bible, for you see, I was the woman caught in adultery.

You see this expensive jewelry I am wearing. You see my fashionable hairdo, and this excess of makeup. Yes, I was a woman of the street. I had many lovers, and they rewarded me for my favors. But only with the things money can buy. They never rewarded me with their love. They wanted my body, not me. But I was too blind to see, too immature to distinguish between passion and love.

I knew it was against the law of Moses. I knew that if caught, I could be stoned to death. But I figured it would never happen to me. Many of my friends did the same thing, yet were always let off easy when they got caught. But it was different with me. Evidently this crowd that started to stone me felt guilty about something they had done, and were trying to cover up by killing me. In the group I recognized some of my lovers. I was so hurt by their hypocrisy that I guess I wanted to die.

Or it could be they were just using me as a pawn to trick Jesus, for they dragged me before him and asked if it was lawful to condemn me to die. Strange as it seems, this unusual teacher didn't answer. He didn't say anything. He just stooped down and wrote something on the ground with his finger, like a child playing. I don't know what he wrote. But the men who saw, quietly slipped out, one by one.

When they were all gone, he merely said, "Go, and sin no more." I was free. Not just free from my executioners, but free from lustful passion. For the first time in my life, I was exposed to love. And now, I am free!

Hymns: "Jesus Is the Friend You Need"
       "Ye Must Be Born Again"
       "Redeemed, How I Love to Proclaim It"

Prayer: We praise thy redeeming power, O Lord, for freeing these men and women from such enemies as greed and passion and death. Today, we are bound by chains, too. The chains may not be made of steel, and they may not bind our wrists and ankles. But they are real, nonetheless. Some of us are bound by prejudices. If so, free us, O God, from feeling we are better than other people and races. Some of us are bound by fear. If so, break its bond with the hammer of faith. Some of us are bound by unconfessed sin, which lies hidden in our breasts. If so, break it with the hammer of thy grace and forgiveness. In the name of the great redeemer and emancipator, Jesus our Lord. Amen.

24 The Living Bible

(*Part I*)

Preparation: At least two devotionals can be planned on this theme. One is given in this chapter, another in the following chapter. The two are not continued, and do not necessarily need to follow one another.

With the ideas in these two chapters as a starter, you could devise for yourself an almost unlimited number of devotionals on objects mentioned in the Bible.

The Bible truly comes alive to us when we see its characters and events in the perspective of today. Let us note four common objects from the Bible, which are also commonplace in our everyday lives. Listen to the message they have for us.

Ladder

(Note: Bring a small ladder or stepladder that can be easily maneuvered.)

There was joy in the home of Isaac and Rebekah when

they became the parents of twin boys: Jacob and Esau. But rivalries and jealousies brought discord into the home. When Jacob obtained the birthright that belonged to Esau, then Esau threatened to kill Jacob. With this threat hanging over his head, Jacob fled for his life.

One of the first nights he was away from home, he camped outdoors, with rocks for a pillow. During the night, he dreamed of a ladder that reached from the ground to heaven. Now it was not a short ladder such as the one we have before us. It must have been tremendous, reaching into the sky. In his dream, Jacob saw angels going up and down the ladder. He dreamed he saw God standing at the top of the ladder. In the vision, God promised to take care of him, to bless him with many children, and to be by his side wherever he went.

We know this dream was fulfilled, because Jacob not only became a prosperous man but later returned to his home and was reunited with Esau.

In his dream, the ladder served to lift his attention from the earth (where he was surrounded by trouble) to heaven. God could have appeared without the aid of the visionary ladder, but it was his way of communicating with the frightened Jacob and lifting his sights and his faith to something greater than himself.

When you and I see a ladder, or use one to paint the ceiling or wash the windows, may it always remind us that there is a heaven as well as an earth. May it cause us momentarily to look up, to be assured there is a higher power than our own, and to know that God is an ever-present source of strength.

I will lift up mine eyes unto the hills, from whence cometh my help. My help cometh from the Lord, which made heaven and earth. . . . Behold, he that keepeth Israel shall neither slumber nor sleep. . . . The Lord shall preserve thy going out and thy coming in from this time forth, and even for evermore (Psalm 121).

Slingshot and Five Rocks

David was the youngest of eight sons of Jesse. Three of his older brothers were away at war, fighting the Philistines. David's father sent him to visit his brothers, and to take them food. While there, Goliath challenged the Israelites, who were about to flee in terror.

Then David volunteered to fight him singlehandedly. Everyone thought this was a joke, but David was serious and reminded them of how successful he had been in killing wild animals which had threatened his flock.

So they fitted him with heavy armor, which he quickly took off. Instead, picking up five smooth stones from a creekbed, he determined to face the giant merely with his sling.

His reason, he said, was to demonstrate that "the Lord saveth not with sword and spear: for the battle is the Lord's, and he will give you into our hands" (1 Sam. 17:47).

I don't know what this sling, which I hold in my hand, says to you today. But to me it is a reminder of the significance of little things.

"For who hath despised the day of small things?" the writer of Zechariah says (4:10).

When Elijah stood on the mountain, fearful that God had forsaken him, he did not find God in a strong earthquake that rent the hills, nor in the wind or fire that followed. Those were dramatic events, and one could conceivably conclude they were evidence of the power and presence of God. Instead, it was the "still small voice" that followed the fire which reassured Elijah of God's nearness.

We look for big headlines, and admire big (important) people, and long for big money, and seek big ways in which to serve God and man. But the little, overlooked factors are often the most meaningful in life.

Remember that, the next time you see a boy's sling!

Lunch Box

This is a lunch box, similar to the one boys and girls often take to school. Now I know there were no lunch boxes such as this in Bible times. But I have brought this lunch box to call attention to a boy's lunch described in John 6:5–13. In their urgency to hear Jesus teach, the multitudes had forgotten to bring bread. Jesus asked the apostles what should be done. Philip pointed out how much it would cost to feed the crowd of five thousand.

It was then that Andrew suggested, "There is a lad here, which hath five barley loaves, and two small fishes." But he went on to apologize that this would not begin to feed those present.

There follows the well-known story of the feeding of the five thousand from this one boy's lunch. Much has been said about the lad's willingness to share, and the Lord's frugality in saving the leftovers. But the central truth is that Christ made much out of little. There is a similarity here to the simple sling that David used to slay Goliath.

You may feel your role in life is small, that your talents

are few. But the degree of dedication is often of greater importance than the size of the gift.

You may pack a simple lunch for that school-age son of yours. It may be an ordinary day in an ordinary week. But on this day he may see a vision of grandeur, a flash of insight to his potential.

In this—and a hundred other ways—you and I can feed the multitudes by using faithfully the small gifts we possess.

Water Bucket and Rope

We don't see many of these around anymore, do we? This may be the first one that many of you have ever seen. Most of us may never have used one.

It is an ordinary metal bucket with a rope tied to the handle. Farm folks used these in large numbers a few years ago, when they drew their water by hand from wells. Sometimes the bucket would double as a make-shift refrigerator. Milk, eggs, and butter were placed in the bucket, and it was lowered into the cool recesses of the well, just above the water level, to keep fresh.

Buckets exactly like this were not used in Bible times to draw water. But they did use some kind of vessel, perhaps a pottery jar, to which was fixed a rope or cord.

With this water bucket as a starter to our imagination, let's visit the little village of Sychar. Let's go at sundown one day, and listen to Jesus who is sitting by the curb of Jacob's well.

Women have come to draw water, and to carry it home on their heads, for this is somewhat of a community well. He engages one of them in conversation, asking for a drink.

She draws back in surprise, for he is a Jew and she a Samaritan. Courteously, Jesus replies that had she asked him, he would have given her a drink—and that she would never have thirsted again!

She points out that the well is deep, and that he has nothing (no bucket or rope) with which to draw water. But he is not referring to water which is two parts hydrogen and one part oxygen (H_2O). He is talking about the refreshing spiritual waters of forgiveness and salvation.

When we want a drink, we turn on the faucet or open the refrigerator. But the water that comes out of today's faucet is no more satisfying than the water that came from Jacob's well. There is still the deep, heart-searching thirst for forgiveness, for spiritual refreshment.

No bucket in the world is big enough to contain that kind of water, and no rope is long enough to reach it. The spiritual water of salvation comes only from God through Christ, but it is as free as the air we breathe if we have faith enough to accept it, and humility enough to acknowledge our need of it.

We don't see many water buckets anymore. But when we do see one, let it be a reminder of our need for the waters from heaven's wells! "If any man thirst, let him come unto me, and drink. He that believeth on me, as the scripture hath said, out of his belly shall flow rivers of living water" (John 7:37–38).

Hymns: "O for a Thousand Tongues"
             "Break Thou the Bread of Life"
             "Truehearted, Wholehearted"

Prayer: Help us to see thy hand, O Lord, in the common things of life—a ladder against a wall, a boy's toy, a glass of water, a simple lunch of bread and fish. Thou hast hidden thyself in the tiny things of life, as well as declared thyself in the glories of eternity. Give us eyes to see thee in both. Amen.

25 The Living Bible

(*Part II*)

Presentation: Before using the suggestions in this chapter, please read the preceding chapter, Part I of "The Living Bible."

A Piece of Handwork

You will notice that I am holding a little girl's skirt (coat, scarf, embroidered piece, or other) that someone has made by hand. Someone cut the material according to a pattern, and sewed and fitted it together.

Assembly-line production has eliminated much of the sewing at home that was a necessity not too many years ago. In Bible times, there were no machines, and all such work was done by hand.

Do you remember a woman in the Bible by the name of Dorcas, or Tabitha? She is described in Acts 9:36–41. About all we know of her is that she was a good woman and a seamstress. Verse 36 says she was "full of good works and almsdeeds." When she died, friends "stood by . . . weeping, and shewing the coats and garments which Dorcas made, while she was with them" (v. 39).

Evidently, she was very generous with what she made, supplying widows and others with articles of clothing. We do not know if she was a woman of prayer, or if she was a leader in the early church, or if she led many people to Christ. All we know is that she did what she could, which was sewing with her hands.

Too often in our churches we try to pour everyone into the same mold. "Anyone can teach a Sunday School class," we say.

But can they? Do all have the same talents? Are all gifted alike? Certainly not.

Martha is often criticized because she spent so much time in the kitchen when Jesus visited her home, while Mary sat at his feet, listening to his teachings. It is true that Jesus commended Mary as doing the better thing. But he did not say that Martha was doing wrong in preparing the meal.

We need Marthas who can scrub and sew and cook, as well as Marys who can sing and pray and teach. But neither is to castigate the other. Let each work within his own ability.

In the immortal tribute to motherhood in Proverbs 31, the writer praises the work of a woman's hands: "She considereth a field, and buyeth it: with the fruit of her hands she planteth a vineyard. She stretcheth out her hand to the poor; yea, she reacheth forth her hands to the needy. She maketh herself coverings of tapestry; her clothing is silk and purple" (vv. 16, 20, 22).

Ten Half-Dollars

Here are ten silver coins. They are probably not as valuable as the ten pieces of silver described in Luke 15:8–10. The story concerns a widow, who lost one of her valuable coins. She lit a candle so as to see in the corners and crevices, swept every inch of her house, and searched in every closet until she found it. Then she invited her neighbors in for a party, and they rejoiced together. "Likewise," Jesus concluded in this parable, "I say unto you, there is joy in the presence of the angels of God over one sinner that repenteth."

The point is that God is just as anxious over a missing sinner as a poverty-stricken widow is over a tenth of her savings. Even more diligently will he seek, and even more joyfully will he rejoice, when that sinner is found.

The next time you drop a coin on the floor or sidewalk and it rolls out of sight, let it say to you that all men without Christ are lost to God, and that the endless, compassionate search for man is never called off, so long as there is any hope or life left.

If you are a Christian, praise the Lord for his relentless search that resulted in bringing you into the fold.

A Piece of Parchment

(You may have to improvise to make this, but the object is to display a roll of heavy paper, supposedly resembling the parchment used for writing in New Testament times.)

When Paul wrote his second letter to Timothy from prison, he closed it by urging Timothy to visit him before winter set in. He reminded him to bring a heavy coat he had left at Troas. He also asked for his books, "but especially the parchments" (2 Tim. 4:13).

In the long days of prison, Paul wanted the books to study, the cloak to keep him warm, and the parchment on which to write letters.

Paul's epistles are more meaningful to us when we realize the difficult situations under which he wrote. He did not use an electric typewriter, nor could he make carbon copies of the letters he wrote to be circulated among the churches. It was long, slow, painstaking work.

Isn't it wonderful that the Word of God has been preserved for us down through the centuries, and that much of it got its start on simple pieces of parchment?

But it is of greater importance that God's Word be written on our hearts and demonstrated in our daily lives. The Word must be written and printed, but the Word must be lived also.

Seven-tiered Candelabra with Candles

As I light these seven candles, I have asked someone to read Revelation 1:12–20:

> And being turned, I saw seven golden candlesticks; And in the midst of the seven candlesticks one like unto the Son of man. . . . His head and his hairs were white like wool, as white as snow; and his eyes were as a flame of fire; . . . the seven candlesticks which thou sawest are the seven churches.

This was a vision John experienced on the Isle of Patmos. He was an old man, and he felt alone and forgotten. But in the vision, he saw Christ active among the candlesticks, the churches.

If you can imagine each of these candles representing a church, and can visualize a spiritual form weaving in and around the seven, you can duplicate his vision. The message is that Christ is with his churches, active among his people.

This suggests the kinship of Christ and his church. Churches have a tremendous responsibility to win, teach, minister, and serve. They are also responsible to keep in touch with the living Christ!

Is this true of our church? Is the flame flickering, or extinguished? Or is it shining brightly, with Christ always near?

Hymns: "Just As I Am"
            "The Solid Rock"

Prayer Suggestion: Use a prayer similar to the format of the one suggested for Part I of this devotional, in the preceding chapter.

26 Power in Storage!

Preparation: Secure dry cell batteries in five different sizes (you may also wish to bring the objects in which they are used): (1) The tiny mercury cell used in a hearing aid (2) A set of four "AA" or penlight cells as used in toys, some transistor radios, some photoflash units; (3) A set of four "C" cells as used in portable tape recorders, etc.; (4) A set of four "D" cells, the familiar flashlight batteries; and (5) A big, six-volt "hot shot" battery, once used for doorbells, now often used for starting model airplanes. (If possible, bring a model airplane to the group. You may be able to borrow one from a hobby shop.)

The World of the Extremely Small

The tiny mercury cell used in a modern hearing aid will operate some of these devices for eighty to one hundred hours. Used in the light meter of a camera, a mercury cell may last a year or more. What is a mercury cell? Is it some magic wand of modern man? No. A mercury cell is a simple battery designed to provide electrical energy when needed.

127

In a general way it accomplishes the same thing the relatively huge storage battery accomplishes in our automobiles. It does its job in a different way, is different in size and in cost, but, basically, it stores power. Not much. Yet, how glorious is the effect of that power to a partially deaf person! This tiny little cell is the means by which the hard-of-hearing may rejoin the wonderful world of sound that otherwise might be closed. Who can measure the value of the blessing?

For the Christian there is another source of unseen power. Romans 15:13 says, "Now the God of hope fill you with all joy and peace in believing, that ye may abound in hope, through the power of the Holy Ghost."

This power can bring both blessings and the necessary control of spiritual life.

Six Volts of Electricity

An "AA" or penlight cell is only two inches long, half an inch in diameter; yet it develops one and one-half volts of electrical power. When four of these tiny cells are connected together in the proper way, six volts are produced. In an electronic flash unit, this power can produce light to rival the brightness of the sun—for 1/2000th of a second, that is! Or the same four cells can operate a transistor radio, power a toy, or supply the energy for a small portable tape recorder. The uses are varied; the power is the same.

Yet, certain rules apply. To give six volts, the four batteries must be connected in series, in such a way as to build on the contribution of each individual cell. We might call this an example of cooperation. If the cells were not so connected, the power of all four would be no greater than the power of a single cell.

The Christian, too, finds that similar rules apply to spiritual power. There is a cooperative power to group prayer; when Christians are "in series" with one another and with God wonderful things happen. Ephesians 3:20 speaks of "the power that worketh in us." The uses the will of God has for this power may be varied; the power itself is the same. And it is not too difficult to see in the tiny "AA" cell resting in a human hand an analogy to our own selves resting in the great hand of God.

Power by Special Design

It is hard to imagine that the big "C" cell contains no more power than the tiny "AA" cell. Yet this is true. Both produce one and one-half volts of direct current. Both can be connected; any combination of four in series would produce the same six volts.

Yet there is a difference.

The *voltage* of the two is the same, but the *amperage,* the total quantity of power, differs. We can think of it this way: There is *more of* the six-volt power in four of the "C" cells than there is in four of the "AA" cells. The trunk of a compact car will carry a load down the highway at 60 miles an hour. The bed of a pickup truck will also carry a load down the highway at 60 miles an hour. The speed is the same, but the load is bigger in the case of the truck. The "C" cells carry a bigger load. They were specially designed for this purpose.

In the same way, Christians are fitted to their jobs. In one sense, all of us do the same job—serve the will of God. But there are times when we need more than "AA" power, times when we need "C" power. The "special design" of God is involved in our lives. Ephesians 4:11 says, "And he gave some, apostles; and some, prophets; and some, evangelists; and some, pastors and teachers."

The Familiar Flashlight Battery

Everyone recognizes the familiar "D" cell. It is what most of us have called the "flashlight battery" most of our lives. It is as familiar to us as the size and shape of a common brick— or a can of beans. Yet this familiar "D" cell, two and one-half times the diameter of the tiny "AA" cell, still produces the same one and one-half volts. Does this not make a good case for democracy in spiritual things? For Christians, too, have different "spiritual diameters" and, yet, often have the same spiritual voltage. Christians, too, often overlook the well-worn and familiar, seeing greater power in something new. Yet the spiritually well-worn and familiar, like the well-worn and familiar flashlight "D" cell, "may produce exactly the same "spiritual voltage" as the exotic, new spiritual thing. Psalm 117:2 says, "The truth of the Lord endureth for ever."

A Big, Square Brute

Is it not strange that the big, square, "hotshot" battery produces the same six volts that four tiny "AA" cells produce? Many of us recall when this was the battery used to power the newfangled doorbells that were used to replace the old pull or turn door alarms that were on Grandmother's front door. These were the batteries used in the "brakeman's lantern" the trainman used to signal the engineer from the rear of the train.

Of all the batteries we have considered, the "hotshot" is the biggest and most impressive. Yet, consider. Which of the ones we have here does the most useful job? It is a hard question to answer, is it not? Certainly, for the hard-of-hearing, the tiny mercury cell is the most important. And it is smaller than one of the terminals of the hotshot!

But it is not fair to compare. After all, the tiny, new dry-cell batteries of today are merely improved versions of the bulkier batteries of the past. In terms of the will of God, the lesson for us is that of adapting to the specific purpose God's will may have for our lives. It is altogether possible that there are times when we may be mercury cells for his will, other times when we may serve as "AA" or "C" or "D" cells. There may even be a few "hotshots" among us the Lord may wish to direct to more useful things!

Hymns: "Power in the Blood"
           "Let Jesus Come into Your Heart"
           "Let Others See Jesus in You"

Prayer: Father God, give us the desire to seek thy will, the wisdom to understand it, the patience to wait out its working in our lives, the courage to change ourselves to match the power requirements of thy kingdom. Like the dry-cell batteries we have just considered, help us to use the energy within our destinies for productive work. For we ask it in the name of Christ. Amen.

27 Get the Picture!

Preparation: Get a Polaroid camera, an ordinary snapshot, a framed picture such as might hang on the wall in your house, a picture from the daily newspaper, a panel from the Sunday comics.

The Instant Image

This may seem an unusual way to begin a devotional. I am going to take your picture. (*Take the Polaroid picture.*) Now, while this is developing, I am going to ask ——— to read Luke 11:33. (*Arrange beforehand for this, so that the person you ask will be prepared.*) In our day, much is made of the "image" we as individuals, the organizations to which we belong, even our nation, makes. What does "image" mean to a Christian?

You have just made this image. This is an instant picture of part of our group. But how truthful an image is it? Certainly it does not show all our group. And it is a picture of us at one particular moment. But it is a picture.

Like many things in our culture, photography is named from the Greek and means literally, "light writing." Light wrote down a record of you. The record is both an image and a story. It can be seen; thus it is an image. But it is also a record written down of an instant of time and, as such, is, in its own way, a story of you as you were when I moved the lever that made the picture.

It seems simple to take such a picture, yet this simple thing involves some extremely complex contributions from the sciences of chemistry and physics. It would take most of us months of study to understand how this happens. So we never bother. We merely snap the picture. Though the image is an instant one, behind it is a very far-reaching science and history.

A Family Memorandum

Here is a snapshot. It is of members of my family. Like the Polaroid picture I just took, it, too, is a story written down by light. But it is different. It captured a moment in the life of my family. It made a memorandum in light and remains, for me, a note to call back that moment, with all its relationships of love and devotion.

Our instant image of a few minutes ago did not tell all the truth about you. It showed you as you were physically in terms of light and shadow. But it could not tell how you felt. It could not give your hopes and dreams and aspirations. It could not go beyond the instant. Yet, the snapshot does. Even though it is no greater an image, because of the way I feel toward these persons, the things I know about them, the relationships we share, this "memorandum of the family" brings back more to me than the bare record of silver salts on paper would indicate.

There is an analogy here to our relationship with God. Those of us who know him, who are close to him, see the world around us as a memorandum of his covenant with man; those who do not know him see it only as an instant image.

Not for nought did the psalmist say in Psalm 19:1: "The heavens declare the glory of God; and the firmament sheweth his handywork."

With Skill and Imagination

This picture is a different kind of record. The skill and imagination of the artist, his long training, the vision he saw in his brain of what the finished picture would be like all combined to make this picture. It is a made thing, but it is a thing of beauty and, as such, is what the poet Keats called it, "a joy forever."

This picture hangs on the wall in my home and gives those who see it pleasure. Great pictures hang in great museums and give all mankind pleasure. In recent years, some builders have invited local artists and painters to paint pictures on the plywood fences that surround construction projects. The skill and imagination may not be that of the greatest artists, but the very fact that there is a colorful picture on the fence reveals that there are those who wish to rise from the commonplace into the extraordinary. God formed man from the dust of the field, the common and the ordinary; but, once the spirit of God was breathed in him and he became a living soul, he was no longer capable of staying on the lowest level. He had been given aspiration.

In a sense, a painting or other work of art is a picture of our hopes and dreams and aspirations, sometimes on a small scale, sometimes on a large one. What do we do with such dreams?

The "Plain Vanilla"

A picture torn from a newspaper page is seldom impressive. The image is coarse, the dots that make up the image smear and blur. After all, nothing about it is supposed to last. A newspaper is just for today.

Yet there is a kind of honesty about the daily newspaper and its pictures that does not exist with other media. The pictures are there for a strictly utilitarian purpose. They are "plain vanilla," but they are honestly so. As such they play their part in our world.

There is an analogy here for the Christian. Much of our living is "plain vanilla" living. It may even be ideal for this to be so. Does not Psalm 18:21 say, "I have kept the ways of the Lord, and have not wickedly departed from my God"?

A More Complete Picture

Of course, the more complete picture for the Christian would include all the elements we have discussed. We are what we are at any particular moment. Life is made up of both dreams and aspirations and the "plain vanilla." Ultimately, of course, the most important part of the picture is our relationship with God. For the Christian this should permeate all existence—from high aspiration to low utility.

Hymns: "Let Others See Jesus in You"
           "Just As I Am"
           "Is Your Life a Channel of Blessing?"

Prayer: Our Father, we thank thee for all the wonders with
            which you have blessed the world. We thank thee
            for the simple and utilitarian things of the world
            we know. We thank thee for the high and lofty
            aspirations thou hast set in our hearts. We thank
            thee most of all for the relationship we may have
            with thee. May we deepen our commitment. May
            we look upon each avenue of service as a means to
            come closer in fellowship with thee. In Jesus'
            name. Amen.